SPEAKING

THEISM, ATE
THE MAGNU.

It were better to have no opinion of God at all than such an opinion as is unworthy of him (FRANCIS BACON)

We no longer think of God as an Atlas; nous n'avons besoin de cet hypothèse (R.M. HARE)

It is a major heresy of post-enlightenment rationalism to try to turn poetry into pseudo-science, to turn the images of religion, whose function is to evoke eternity, into mundane description of improbable facts (KEITH WARD)

God is in no way like the things that have being and we have no knowledge at all of his incomprehensible and ineffable transcendence and invisibility (PSEUDO-DIONYSIUS)

SPEAKING OF GOD
Theism, Atheism &
The Magnus Image

T. R. Miles

William Sessions Limited
York, England

ISBN 1 85072 202 1

Printed in 11 on 12½ point Plantin typeface
from Author's Disk
by Sessions of York
The Ebor Press
York, England

Contents

Preface

THE TITLE OF THIS BOOK – which was arrived at only after several false starts – calls for some explanation. Basically I shall be trying to come to terms with a paradox, viz. that people can and do speak of God even though in strictness there is nothing which can be said. My purpose is in effect to commend a particular view of the role and function of religious language. In doing so I shall try to correct, in both myself and others, what I believe to be some erroneous assumptions which underlie popular talk – and, indeed, sometimes learned talk – on the subject of 'theism' and 'atheism'.

The sub-title also refers – somewhat cryptically – to 'the Magnus image'; and I should like to indicate how this expression arose. What initially sparked me off nearly thirty years ago was a comment made by Alasdair MacIntyre in connection with John Robinson's book, *Honest to God* (Preface note 1). According to MacIntyre 'what is striking about Dr Robinson's book is first and foremost that he is an atheist' (Preface note 2). This remark produced a rejoinder by Don Cupitt: 'If *Honest to God* were really atheistic, it is a little surprising that it should have converted so many people to Christianity' (Preface note 3). Cupitt, too, has been called an atheist. According to a Sunday newspaper it has been said by 'a liberal minded bishop' that 'one of the big questions we have to face is what is to be done about the thorough-going atheism of Don Cupitt' (Preface note 4).

All this seems very strange. Surely, one might say, people *know* whether they are atheists or not – and if they are atheists how can they also be ordained clergymen?

This gave me the idea that what Robinson, Cupitt, and others were rejecting could be termed 'the Magnus image' – a sort of popular conception of God which portrays God as a being who 'exists' in an entirely literal sense. A central theme of the present book is that in current religious thinking the words 'theism' and 'atheism' are often tied to the

vi

Magnus image, whereas my argument is – to dress a logical point in figurative language – that Magnus needs to be dethroned. This was in effect the view of Robinson, who wrote in reply to MacIntyre:

> Perhaps, as part of his protest against the current trivialisation of God, a Christian has to be prepared to be called an atheist...If God is equated with a supernatural Being whose existence over and above the world has to be demonstrated, I am not prepared to spend time defending the charge (Preface note 5).

Cupitt's ideas are similar. In one of his books, which he entitled *Taking Leave of God* (Preface note 6), there is on the fly-leaf a quotation from Eckhart which runs:

> Man's last and highest parting occurs when, for God's sake, he takes leave of God.

The crucial words here seem to me to be 'highest' and 'for God's sake'. To 'take leave' of a very limited conception of God is not the abandonment of religious commitment which the word 'atheism' is often thought to imply.

In general, therefore, it seems to me clear that those ordained ministers whose views are similar to those of Robinson and Cupitt are not atheistic in any sense that would require them to give up the priesthood. As will be indicated further in Chapter 3, what they are rejecting is not a set of timeless truths which have always been part of the Christian tradition but some highly questionable formulations which are largely a consequence of post-16th century thinking in western Europe.

One of my central aims is therefore to call attention to the absurdity of discussing religious issues in 'Magnus' terms. If my view of religious language is correct it follows, not, as I once supposed, that all disputes between so-called 'theists' and so-called 'atheists' disappear, but that they need to be seen in a new light. Indirectly the book is also a plea for religious tolerance – not simply because such tolerance is a good thing in general but because *from the very nature of religious language* there cannot be the same certainties as belong, for instance, in the area of mathematical proof and as are regularly found both in science and in common sense observation. Religious language is not *inferior* to other kinds of language but it is *different*; and, in my judgment, some present day thinkers have failed adequately to emphasise the relevant differences. In particular it needs to be noted that there is not the same logical justification for telling people that their religious views are mistaken as there is for telling them that they are mistaken over any of these other issues.

The consequence, however, is not that readers need change their religious practices, though I should like to think that as a result of my arguments they will carry out these practices with increased understanding and – in view of the very nature of religious language – with increased tolerance for the views of others.

This being the case, it is of course not my intention to impose my personal religious views on any of my readers. I am in fact a member of the Society of Friends (Quakers), but my hope is that the arguments presented in this book will be of interest to people of many religious beliefs and indeed to people who profess no religious belief at all.

I owe much to the influence of my philosophical mentor, Gilbert Ryle, and I have also been particularly helped by the writings of John Robinson and Don Cupitt. Others who have influenced me have been Donald Mackinnon, Ian Ramsey, Richard Hare, Hywel Lewis, George Hughes, Dewi Phillips, and Dick Milford. I am grateful to Don Cupitt, Martin Warner, Stephen Mitchell, Mark Williams, John Challenor, Dafydd Wynn Parry, and Jack Moore for reading various draft versions of the book and for making many helpful suggestions. I should like to thank William Sessions, my publishers, and Richard York in particular, for their help both with the book's title and in many other ways. Finally I am grateful to my Quaker friends, Lorna Marsden, Gerald Richards, Ian Grimsdale, and David Murray-Rust not only for their comments but also for their encouragement when the book had barely begun to take shape. For the book's shortcomings I alone am responsible.

T.R.M.

Bangor, 1997

Postscript

The notes which accompany each chapter have the following purposes: (i) to provide references for the quotations given in the main text; (ii) to call attention to a number of philosophical technicalities which would cause unnecessary complication if they occurred in the main body of the text, and (iii) to add some incidental comments, mostly of a personal or light-hearted kind.

CHAPTER 1

Standard truths and profound truths

IN A CHARACTERISTICALLY witty passage towards the end of the introduction to *The Concept of Mind* (note 1.1) Gilbert Ryle wrote:

> Some readers may think that my tone of voice in this book is excessively polemical. It may comfort them to know that the assumptions against which I exhibit most heat are assumptions of which I myself have been a victim. Primarily I am trying to get some disorders out of my own system. Only secondarily do I hope to help other theorists to recognise our malady and to benefit from my medicine.

In this book my approach will be similar. I have no wish to tell other people how wrong they are (note 1.2); my aim is rather to invite others to join me on an exploration. I am interested in trying to specify what should be the characteristics of any language which merits the description 'religious'.

A distinction which is fundamental to the book is that between *standard truths* and *profound truths*. I shall try to show that the ways in which we discuss the former are crucially different from the ways in which we discuss the latter. It is one of my main theses that the apparent conflict between 'theism' and 'atheism' has arisen because these two kinds of truth have not been adequately distinguished.

The distinction which I have in mind can best be illustrated by means of examples. The following, at least in normal circumstances, are examples of standard truth: (i) '2+2=4', (ii) 'There is

1

some cheese in the cupboard', (iii) 'Action and reaction are equal and opposite', (iv) 'All mammals have backbones'.

In contrast it is a characteristic of profound truth that it involves reflection on issues which have to do with life, death, and human destiny. For instance there is a stanza from Edward Fitzgerald's translation of the *Rubaiyat of Omar Khayyam.* which runs:

> Into this Universe, and *why* not knowing,
> Nor *whence*, like Water willy-nilly flowing:
> And out of it, as Wind along the Waste,
> I know not *whither*, willy-nilly blowing (note 1.3).

As a further example I should like to quote the well-known stanza from Emily Brontë's *Last Lines*:

> Vain are the thousand creeds
> That move men's hearts: unutterably vain;
> Worthless as wither'd weeds,
> Or idlest froth amid the boundless main,
> To waken doubt in one
> Holding so fast by Thine infinity;
> So surely anchor'd on
> The steadfast rock of immortality (note 1.4)

Finally, let me quote the following biblical passage:

> Before Abraham was, I am (note 1.5).

I am not, of course, offering here any clear-cut formula by which profound truths can be differentiated from standard truths; and, as with many proposals for classification, there may be ambiguous or borderline cases. However the above examples will, I hope, make clear the distinction which I have in mind.

It is a characteristic of profound language that the rules inherent in standard language are sometimes intentionally violated so as to produce a particular effect or insight – as in the case of 'Before Abraham was, I am'; and often profound language is so rich in meaning that it is possible to interpret it at many different levels, as in:

> the water that I shall give him shall be in him a well of
> water springing up into everlasting life (note 1.6).

Sometimes, too, though not invariably, profound truths are expressed through the medium of poetry

The central theme of the book is that *religious language should always be understood as conveying profound truth and not standard truth.*

Now an important sub-group among standard truths are those which refer to issues of fact (in a sense to be discussed further in Chapter 4). Examples of issues of fact are whether fairies exist, whether there is a monster in the depths of Loch Ness, or whether there are trams in Sheffield. One of my central themes is that it is a mistake to assimilate the question of 'whether God exists' to factual questions of this kind. As far as I know, fairies do not exist; there is not a monster in the depths of Loch Ness, and there are trams in Sheffield. What I shall be challenging in this book is the assumption that 'the existence of God' is an issue of a similar kind or, for those that prefer the philosophical term, that it is an issue of the same logical type.

At this point I should perhaps make clear that nowhere in the book will I be expressing any views as to how the evidence in a given area needs to be evaluated. My enquiry is what philosophers have called a 'second order' one: I shall be asking, not whether a particular statement is true or false, but what job – what function – the words in question are, or should be, performing. I shall suggest that we should think of profound truths as having a different 'logic' from standard truths, which is to say in effect that the ways in which we need to discuss them are different. Wittgenstein in his philosophical writings (note 1.7) suggested a comparison between using language and following the rules of a game. If one adopts Wittgenstein's picture one can say that different 'language games' have different 'rules'. Of course one of the striking things about profound language is that the 'rules' (if they can be so called) are more flexible than in the case of standard language; one's job is not necessarily to aim at intellectual understanding but rather to listen and perhaps hope that that in consequence some new insight will be gained or, in popular parlance, that 'the penny will drop' (note 1.8). If particular words in profound language do not 'speak to' a given individual the issue is not one for logical argument.

To determine what are the facts one examines evidence. If the evidence is ambiguous one does the best one can; and if fresh evidence comes to light one has the duty to examine it and possibly to change one's mind. This, however, is not the way in which it is appropriate to discuss profound truths – and therefore the truths of religion. Indeed, as I shall try to show in subsequent chapters, a religious commitment may sometimes be one which is adhered to *in spite of* the facts being what they are. The central thesis of this book is that those who argue about the existence of God as though it were an issue of fact are degrading religion – and are making the mistake of confusing profound truth with standard truth.

I propose to end this discussion of profound and standard truth in a lighter vein. There is a superb passage in that great master of English prose, P.G. Wodehouse, in which an elderly soldier fails to recognise – as I would put the matter – the difference between the two:

> 'I mean', said Freddie, who felt strongly on the subject, it's love that makes the world go round. 'It isn't anything of the kind,' said Sir Aylmer. Like so many fine old soldiers he was inclined to be a little literal-minded. 'I never heard such dashed silly nonsense in my life. What makes the world go round is .... Well, I've forgotten at the moment, but it certainly isn't love. How the dooce could it?' ......

A little later there was the following exchange:

> 'Ah, well, all flesh is as grass'. 'No, it isn't. It's nothing of the kind. The two things are entirely different. I've seen flesh and I've seen grass. No resemblance whatever' (note 1.9).

I am tempted to suggest that some present-day discussions of religious issues are conducted with the same literal-mindedness as that displayed in the above passages by Sir Aylmer.

Finally, I should like to introduce the reader to an idea which is central to the whole book. This central point is that if we discuss 'the existence of God' as if it was an issue of fact then we are in bondage to what I call 'the "Magnus" image'. Let me explain.

4

'Magnus' is the Latin for 'big' or 'great'. What many of us – myself included – have been tempted to suppose is that one can legitimately argue as to whether there is in fact a 'big' or 'great' person who made the universe and who is now in charge of it. The existence of such a being is as much an issue of fact as whether there is a monster in the depths of Loch Ness. I am not, of course, talking about a bearded figure who sits on the clouds, since any thoughtful person professing to be a 'theist' would reject such a picture. What I have in mind by 'the Magnus image' is something much more sophisticated than this – a being who, though not visible or tangible, *really does exist* (note 1.10). Magnus, as I shall be explaining more fully in later chapters, has therefore to be thought of as a 'non-material' or 'non-physical' being. This means that he is not made of 'matter', though, since he made the 'material' world, some interaction between the 'non-material' and the 'material' must at some time have taken place. I also characterise him as a 'supernatural' being, since he falls outside the so-called 'natural order' of causes and effects (note 1.11). In accordance with common assumptions I have also characterised him as being male.

I shall argue that many of the apparently irreconcilable disputes over 'the existence of God' have arisen because the issues have been presented in 'Magnus' terms. What I want to put in the place of such disputes is an appreciation of the *profundity* of religious language and a plea for 'the way of silence'. This latter is in effect a recognition that any attempt to express religious truths in words must in the last resort be inadequate. This idea has played a significant part in Christian thinking in the past but has largely been neglected by some of the theologians and philosophers of religion whose work I refer to in this book.

In chapter 2 I shall present some passages from Greek, Roman, Hebrew, and early Christian traditions which I hope will convince readers that the idea of a 'supernatural' or 'non-material' being is largely absent. In Chapter 3 I shall indicate the historical context in which 'Magnus' ways of thinking took shape; and I shall try to show that these ways of thinking, so far from being eternal truths, are the product of certain ideas in our western civilisation that took shape during the last few hindred years. Those who reject the Magnus image, therefore, are not just a group of maverick

5

'modernists'; rather they are thinkers who refuse to be tied by some highly questionable assumptions which go back no earlier than about the 16th century.

Since one of the points to be discussed is whether – or in what sense – 'the existence of God' is an issue of fact Chapter 4 will contain some philosophical discussion which attempts to elucidate the words 'exist' and 'fact' and the related word 'real'.

In chapter 5 I shall try to make explicit why exactly it is that thinking in 'Magnus' terms is an error. In this chapter I lead readers by small stages from the admission – which they are unlikely to query – that the words 'right hand of God' are not to be taken literally to the recognition that the words 'real', 'exist', and 'causes things to happen' cannot be taken literally either. In chapter 6 I shall call attention to the way in which we argue about issues of fact – about the rules of this particular 'language game' (see note 1.7). The problem is this: given that Magnus is 'immaterial' and 'invisible', we are in danger of being misled by an inappropriate analogy, that of the 'hidden puppeteer'. If puppets are seen to be moving it is reasonable to suppose that someone behind the scenes is pulling the strings, and the pay-off observation occurs when one goes behind the stage and meets the puppeteer. It is self-defeating, however, to use words which imply that someone behind it all is 'there' if one does not specify what is meant by 'there' and what would count as the 'pay off' observation which would clinch the matter.

I shall argue in chapter 7 that the alternative to 'Magnus' ways of thinking is 'the way of silence' – the 'apophatic' or negative way (note 1.12). At this point I shall also introduce the term 'mythos', a mythos being a way of expressing profound truth in the language of standard truth – language which will therefore mislead if taken literally.

In chapter 8 I shall try to exhibit some of the uncomfortable consequences of viewing prayer in 'Magnus' terms, and I shall do the same in respect of miracles in chapter 9 and in respect of various traditional Christian doctrines in chapter 10. I shall be commending instead 'the way of silence'. In chapter 11 I shall argue that rejection of the Magnus image can exhibit the so-called 'problem of evil' in something of a new light. Finally, in chapter 12 I shall suggest that since the very asking of the question, 'Does God exist?' presupposes 'Magnus' ways of thinking the case is now very strong for leaving such disputes behind us. If we recognise the need for silence it is possible to move *beyond* theism and atheism – although, as I shall try to show, this recognition does not commit people to any change in their religious practices.

CHAPTER 2

Nature and super-nature: the material and the non-material

I HAVE INTRODUCED what I have called 'the Magnus image' as a way of trying to rid myself of a tempting – yet false – thesis. This thesis is that the crucial religious issue for our time is whether there exists a supernatural or non-material entity, God, who in an entirely literal sense created the universe. The popular account is that if one believes such a being exists one is a 'theist'; if one believes that no such being exists one is an 'atheist', while if one reserves judgment one is an 'agnostic'.

It is all too easy to suppose that the question of God's 'existence' (in this sense) is one among a small number of 'ultimate' questions which have remained the same over the centuries and are asked in all parts of the world. They hang around, in the words of my former tutor, T.D. Weldon, 'like incomplete crossword puzzles set by God to baffle successive generations' (note 2.1). In contrast I shall argue that 'Magnus' ways of thinking are seldom found before the 16th century and that – since nowadays it is difficult to discuss 'the existence of God' except in 'Magnus' terms – we can increase our religious awareness by moving 'beyond theism and atheism' (which is the title of chapter 12 of this book). As I shall be making clear throughout, such a change in awareness need in no way commit anyone to changing their religious practices.

As a corrective to 'Magnus' ways of thinking we need to recognise that religious language takes many different forms in different parts of the world. In this chapter I shall be discussing only western ways of thinking. Even with this limitation, however, it seems plain that the language games played over the past three millennia have been extremely diverse. I propose, therefore, to invite the reader to accompany me on a journey in which we shall briefly survey some of the many influences – Greek, Roman, Hebrew, and early Christian – which have shaped people's religious beliefs during this period. I shall show that 'Magnus' ways of thinking are almost wholly absent: in particular one hears nothing at all of any contrast between the 'natural' and the 'supernatural' and very little of the contrast between the 'material' and the 'non-material'. It is highly significant, in my view, that if one looks up the word 'supernatural' in Cruden's *Concordance* to the bible (note 2.2) there is no entry whatever.

If, as our starting point, we consider the gods and goddesses of ancient Greece, we do indeed find that according to the early myths they were credited with extraordinary powers; for example on one occasion Pallas Athene turned herself into a vulture (note 2.3), while, according to sundry sources, Zeus (for various reasons which we need not go into) turned himself into a bull, a shower of gold, and a swan. There was clearly an awareness, therefore, of what could normally be expected of human beings and a corresponding recognition that the gods could do exceptional things. A sub-division, however, into those events which conformed to natural law and those events which did not was clearly foreign to Greek thinking, and there is no easy way by which the word 'supernatural', in its present-day sense, can be translated into Greek.

Nor were the gods and goddesses 'non-material' beings. At times they actually fought with each other, and it is hard to see how a non-material being – presumably some kind of insubstantial shadow – could be effective in a fight! For example this is the scene as depicted by Homer (note 2.4):

> Such was the turmoil as the battle of the gods began. And little wonder, when the Lord Poseidon was faced by Phoebus Apollo with his winged arrows, and Athene of the Flashing Eyes by Ares; when Here was confronted by Apollo's sister, Artemis of the Golden Distaff...Leto by the formidable Hermes, Bringer of Luck; and Hephaestus by the mighty swirling River who is called Xanthus...

9

Sometimes, too, they indulged in intrigue, as on the celebrated occasion when Ares and Aphrodite were discovered in bed together by Aphrodite's husband, Hephaestus (note 2.5). Nothing immaterial here! Pallas Athene was able to cause a missile to miss its mark (note 2.6), but there is no suggestion that she achieved this by what we would now call 'psychokinesis' – which is understood to mean 'the power of mind over matter'.

Nor in Homer does the word 'psyche' – though standardly translated as 'soul' – imply anything 'immaterial'. When a warrior was killed in the Trojan war his psyche left his body through the wound and went to Hades, the land of the dead. Thus when Hector was killed by Achilles we are told:

> Death cut Hector short and from his limbs his psyche took wing for Hades, bewailing its lot and the youth and manhood that it left (note 2.7).

Moreover those in Hades had only a 'shadowy' or 'dreamlike' existence. The following are the words of Odysseus who, though living, had the opportunity to visit the underworld:

> I mused in my heart and would fain have embraced the spirit of my mother dead. Thrice I sprang towards her, and was minded to embrace her; thrice she flitted from my hands as a shadow or even as a dream (note 2.8)

Shadows and dreams were no doubt familiar enough, but there is no suggestion here of a contrast between the 'material' and the 'non-material'.

It is only when we come to Plato's *Phaedo* that anything resembling such a contrast can be found. In this dialogue Socrates asserts that in certain conditions the psyche

> departs to the place where things are like itself – invisible, divine, immortal and wise (note 2.9)

Even here, however, it is difficult to be sure what Plato - or possibly Socrates – had in mind; and I think it would be widely agreed by scholars that although there is some justification for characterising Plato as a 'dualist' the *Phaedo* is not typical of Greek thought in general.

In Aristotle the psyche is what makes living beings alive (note 2.10):

That which is be-souled ('empsychon') differs from that which is soulless (a-psychon) by being alive.

Even plants have 'a psyche of a kind' since they can take in nourishment. Although some of Aristotle's ideas are hard to interpret, it is clear that he does not think of the psyche as an 'immaterial entity' existing in isolation from the body. Since the mediaeval theologians – including Aquinas in particular – followed Aristotle rather than Plato, 'dualist' ideas formed only a relatively minor part of Christian thinking.

If we now turn to the Roman world of the first century B.C. we again find nothing suggestive of a distinction between the 'material' and the 'non-material'. When Lucretius discusses the gods he agrees that their nature is *tenvis* (approximately 'flimsy') and 'eludes the touch and pressure of our hands' (note 2.11). However this is by no means the same as saying that they are 'non-material', and it would in fact be very hard to find a Latin word which adequately expresses this idea. Lucretius does indeed use the words 'animus' and 'anima', and, *faute de mieux*, many translators have had recourse to the words 'mind' and 'soul'. However a translation which does justice to the original ideas is virtually impossible.

The animus, which we often call the *mens* (intellect), in which the guidance and control of life reside, is part a person no less than hand, foot, or eye... Next you must understand that there is *anima* in our limbs... Life often lingers in our limbs after a large part of the body has been cut off. On the other hand, when a few particles of heat have dispersed and some air has been let out through the mouth life forsakes the veins forthwith and abandons the bones...It is chiefly thanks to the atoms of wind and heat that life lingers in the limbs... (The *animus*) is as it were the head (*caput*) and dominant force in the whole body...It is firmly lodged in the mid-region of the breast... The rest of the *anima*, diffused throughout the body, obeys the *animus* and moves under its direction and impulse... The same

11

> reasoning proves that the *animus* and the *anima* are both corporeal (pertaining to body)... My next task will be to demonstrate to you what sort of body it is... It is of very fine texture and composed of exceptionally minute particles (note 2.12).

Lucretius argues elsewhere (note 2.13) that the world consists of atoms and void, but again there is no suggestion that it consists both of 'material' stuff and of 'non-material' or 'spiritual' stuff.

We also find in Lucretius a concept not far removed from what we would now call 'laws of nature'. Following his mentor, Epicurus, he was at pains to point out that things did not just happen randomly and that there was no need to fear arbitrary punishments from the gods.

> When human life lay grovelling ... crushed to the earth under the dead weight of superstition... a man of Greece {Epicurus} was first to raise mortal eyes in defiance... He proclaimed to us what can be and what cannot: how a limit is fixed to the power of everything and an immovable frontier point. Therefore superstition in its turn lies crushed beneath his feet, and we by his triumph are lofted level with the skies (note 2.14).

At a stretch, therefore, one could say that in this passage Lucretius was drawing a distinction between the 'natural' and the 'supernatural', but he was certainly not doing so in as many words.

If we now turn to Hebrew thought one of the first things we notice was the connection between life and the ability to breathe. We learn from *Genesis* that when God created man he 'breathed into his nostrils the breath of life; and man became a living soul' (note 2.15). Similarly, when Ezekiel described his vision of the valley of dry bones he noted that the bones had 'no breath in them'; and it was only when the four winds breathed upon them that they became alive (note 2.16).

At no point in the Old or New Testaments was Jehovah thought of as a 'non-material' being. We find a wealth of images: he could be jealous (note 2.17); he sits between the cherubims (note 2.18), and before him 'the nations are as a drop of a bucket' (note 2.19).

12

Above all, he was holy and righteous, and one could not look on his face and live.

> Then said I, Woe is me! for I am undone; because I am a man of unclean lips and I dwell in the midst of a people of unclean lips: for mine eyes have seen the king, the LORD of hosts (note 2.20)

We are told, of course, that 'the fool hath said in his heart "There is no god"' (note 2.21); and at first glance this may seem like a posing of the problem in 'Magnus' terms. Certainly one cannot rule out the idea that the Jews in the centuries before Christ had something approximately corresponding to a 'Magnus' problem – a literal view of God, in contrast with the view that his name was too holy to mention. However there was nothing in their conception of God which would have led them to think of him as a 'non-material' or 'supernatural' being; this, as I shall argue in Chapter 3, reflects post-16th century ways of thinking and would have made no sense in the era which we are now considering. Similarly when later Jewish thinking came under the influence of Greek ideas it was possible to identify God with the 'logos' (note 2.22), but there was no suggestion that the logos was 'immaterial' or 'non-physical'.

If we turn now to the Greek of the new testament we do, indeed, find regular uses for the word 'psyche' – approximately equivalent to the Latin 'animus'. This still does not mean, however, that people thought in terms of an 'immaterial substance' or of something that was 'non-physical'. Thus when we are told, 'Love the Lord thy God with all thy heart, and with all thy soul, and with all thy mind, and with all thy strength' (note 2.23), this should not be understood as a kind of roll-call of parts of our personality which can be differentiated: it does not mean that three different kinds of love are called for, viz. heart-love, soul-love, and mind-love; what is implied is a call for commitment with our whole being. Similarly in St. Matthew's gospel we read, 'Fear him which is able to destroy both soul (psyche) and body (soma) in hell' (note 2.24). Translation of 'psyche' as 'soul' is perhaps unavoidable; but if we then think of the soul as an immaterial substance we are being misled by ways of thinking which did not arise until many centuries later.

The well known passage 1 Corinthians (note 2.25) is particularly interesting in this connection. The image is one of sowing:

> That which thou sowest, thou sowest not that body that shall be, but bare grain... So also is the resurrection of the dead. It is sown in corruption; it is raised in incorruption... It is sown a natural body (psychikon soma); it is raised a spiritual body (pneumatikon soma).

The word 'pneumatikon' must undoubtedly have had all sorts of interesting associations for those who read the text in the Greek. 'Pneuma' means 'wind' or 'breath' and 'hagion pneuma' meant 'Holy Spirit'. What we must emphatically not suppose is that the word 'psyche' means 'soul' in the sense of a 'non-physical' entity which survives death. A psyche, as we have seen, is what makes living things alive, and it is interesting that the New English Bible translates 'psychikon soma' as 'animal body'.

There are, of course, references in the new testament to what is 'unseen'. Thus faith is said to be 'the substance of things hoped for, the evidence of things not seen' (note 2.26). Similarly we read that 'the things which are seen are temporal; but the things which are not seen are eternal' (note 2.27). It by no means follows, however, that things which one cannot see should therefore be thought of as 'non-material'. We are also told that 'they that are after the flesh do mind the things of the flesh; but they that are after the Spirit the things of the Spirit' (note 2.28). Here the Greek words are 'sarx' (flesh) and 'pneuma' (spirit); but there is no reason to suppose that this implies a contrast between the 'material' and the 'non-material'.

To sum up, there is little evidence that among the ancient Greeks or in Roman or Hebrew thought in the centuries around the start of the Christian era people discussed problems of religion in terms of whether entities or beings existed who were 'supernatural' or 'non-material'. As I have chosen to put the matter, there was little evidence of 'Magnus' ways of thinking. It follows that those thinkers of the present time who have challenged the need to think of religious commitment in this way cannot be accused of disbelieving what all other Christians have believed through the ages. On the contrary, as I shall try to show in the next chapter, what they are rejecting is a post-16th-century accretion which – so far from being basic to Christianity – has arguably influenced western thought for the worse.

CHAPTER 3

Magnus as a post-16th-century invention

MAGNUS HAS BEEN CHARACTERISED as a being who is 'super-natural' and 'non-material'. I shall argue in this chapter that the question whether a Magnus-like being exists, so far from being one of the eternally challenging questions for all time, is in fact the product of a particular intellectual Zeitgeist which existed in the western world from about the 16th century A.D. onwards.

It was noted in the last chapter that in Cruden's *Concordance to the Bible* (note 3.1) there was no entry under the word 'super-natural'. It seemed to me that it might also be interesting to check how often the word 'supernatural' occurred in Shakespeare (note 3.2) and what were the earliest uses reported in the *Oxford English Dictionary*.

In Shakespeare the word occurs only twice. One of the passages is in *Macbeth* (Act 1, scene 4) ('This supernatural soliciting cannot be ill'), the other in *All's Well that Ends Well* ('Things supernatural and causeless'). There are of course plenty of happenings displayed on stage which we would *now* call 'supernatural – for instance the appearance of ghosts (Banquo, Julius Caesar, Hamlet's father, Richard III's victims), and the disappearance of the banquet in *The Tempest*. They are not, however, described as 'supernatural' by Shakespeare himself.

The entries under the word 'supernatural' in the *Oxford English Dictionary* show an interesting evolution. The earliest of them have nothing to do with religion. They include, for instance, 'Unnaturall or supernaturall heate distrayeth appetite' (1533) and 'Conserninge the supernaturall teeth, it is sometimes daungerous to draw them' (1594). It was not until the late 19th century that there was any suggestion that 'supernatural' events might be regarded as violations of the laws of nature. At this point one finds: 'The Apostles considered supernatural power as something resident in Jesus' (1892), and 'When the Word was made Flesh, a supernatural Being entered what we call the order of nature' (1907).

It was in this context, so I am suggesting, that the Magnus image was born. People came to believe that a distinction could be drawn between the 'supernatural' and the 'natural' and between the 'non-material' and the 'material'. God had to be thought of as a supernatural and non-material being.

They then went on to assume that these two pairs of terms provided a criterion for judging who should be counted as 'religious': to be religious one had to believe in supernatural and non-material entities, whereas the non-religious person believed only in 'natural' and 'material' ones.

Here is a passage from Descartes (1596-1650) which in many ways reflects the mood of his time since it reflects both advances in technology and the importance which was now being attached to 'physical' or 'mechanical' explanations:

> You may have seen in grottoes and fountains in royal gardens that the force with which the water moves, in passing from the spring, is on its own enough to move various machines, and even to make them play on instruments, or utter words, according to the different arrangement of the pipes which conduct it. And indeed the nerves of the machine (sc. an animal body) which I am describing to you may very well be compared to the pipes of the machinery of these fountains, its muscles and its tendons to various other engines and devices which serve to move them, its animal spirits to the water which sets them in motion, of which the heart is the spring and the cavities of the brain the outlets.....Finally, when the reasonable soul shall be in this machine, it will be there like the fountain maker, who must be at the

openings where all the pipes of these machines discharge themselves, if he wishes to start, to stop, or to change in any way their movements (note 3.3).

This is not, of course, simply a 'materialist' picture. Descartes believed not only that the world contained forces which interacted mechanically but that there was also a 'mind' or 'soul' which is 'wholly distinct from the body' (note 3.4). 'Mind' and 'matter' were thus two distinct kinds of reality – 'mind' being something 'non-material – , and their nature and interrelationship was debated by philosophers for the next three centuries.

What was also happening was a recognition that the methods of scientific experimentation could lead to a massive increase in our power over the world around us. Here is Kant's account, written in the 18th century, of how physical science became firmly established as a valid discipline:

When Galileo experimented with balls of a definite weight on the inclined plane, when Torricelli caused the air to sustain a weight which he had calculated beforehand to be equal to that of a definite volume of water... a light broke upon all natural philosophers...Accidental observations, made according to no preconceived plan, cannot be united under a necessary law... Reason must approach nature... not...in the character of a pupil who listens to all that his master chooses to tell him, but in that of a judge, who compels the witnesses to reply to those questions which he thinks fit to propose. To this single idea must the revolution be ascribed, by which, after groping in the dark for so many centuries, natural science was at length conducted into the path of certain progress (note 3.5).

In brief, there was a breakthrough in natural science because it was recognised that the laws of nature were open to systematic examination. In contrast, as Kant emphasised, no such certainty was possible over the issues of God, freedom, and immortality (note 3.6).

Now it is widely agreed among present-day philosophers that to talk of '*the* mind' and '*the* body' is a mistake. Here is Gilbert Ryle's account of how philosophy went wrong (note 3.7):

17

When Galileo showed that his methods of scientific discovery were competent to provide a mechanical theory which should cover every occupant of space, Descartes found in himself two conflicting motives. As a man of scientific genius he could not but endorse the claims of mechanics, yet as a religious and moral man he could not accept... the discouraging rider to these claims, namely that human nature differs only in degree of complexity from clockwork... He and subsequent philosophers naturally but erroneously availed themselves of the following escape-route. Since mental-conduct words are not to be construed as signifying the occurrence of mechanical processes, they must be construed as signifying the existence of non-mechanical processes...Still unwittingly adhering to the grammar of mechanics (Descartes) tried to avert disaster by describing minds in what was merely an obverse vocabulary. The workings of minds had to be described by the mere negatives of the specific descriptions given to bodies: they are not in space, they are not motions, they are not modifications of matter, they are not accessible to public observation. Minds are not bits of clockwork, they are just bits of not-clockwork.

Many of those who have said that they disagree with Ryle's philosophy have in my view misunderstood him (note 3.8). He in fact says virtually nothing about religious beliefs, apart from saying that those who have accepted the 'theory of mind' which he is attacking have included religious thinkers (note 3.9). However it is unnecessary for purposes of this book to insist that one philosophical view about the 'mind-body' group of problems is right as against any other. I wish to claim only that religious thinking does not have to be cast in dualist or 'Magnus' terms: in other words, the idea that God is a 'supernatural' 'non-material' or being is not a timeless truth which from the beginning Christians were required to accept but a highly questionable product of post-16th century thinking.

To sum up, I have characterised Magnus in terms of two distinctions – that between the 'natural' and the 'supernatural' and

18

that between the 'material' and the 'non-material'. The mistake which I have set myself to expose in this book is the supposition that unless one believes in the existence of a Magnus-like being defined in this way, one cannot be a committed Christian.

I end this chapter with a series of intentionally ironic comments.

Physical forces may seem to be all that there is, but may it not be that there are *non-physical* (or Magnus-like) forces in addition? The physical world could have existed from all eternity, but one possibility is that there was a piece of non-physical activity by a non-physical Being, viz. Magnus, which set things going. Moreover, although matter is subject to laws which apply most of the time, it is possible that in the years following creation Magnus decided that from time to time he might usefully intervene and prevent these laws from operating. In that case one must say that, in addition to the *natural* forces which we regularly find to be at work there are also *supernatural* ones which come into play on special occasions; and when they do so the result is said to be a *miracle*. Besides doing all this, Magnus also created human souls, which, like himself, are non-physical substances and therefore not subject to the laws of 'matter'; and this means that it is possible for them to survive the dissolution of the body (a 'material thing') at death. Moreover, on the assumption that they are subject to the laws of physics it follows that there can be no freedom of choice but only the inexorable march of blind mechanical forces. The human being, on this showing, is simply

> just a being that moves
> in predestinate grooves,
> not a taxi or bus, but a tram (note 3.10).

Free will, it seems, – along with a religious view of mankind in general – can be saved only if one postulates the existence of non-material forces as well as material ones.

I shall argue in what follows that presenting the issues in this way is both degrading to religion and the consequence of using words in a self-defeating way.

19

CHAPTER 4

Reality, existence, and issues of fact

MAGNUS HAS BEEN DEFINED in such a way that the question of whether or not he *exists* is assumed to be an issue of fact. Although it is not my intention in this book to introduce any large number of philosophical technicalities the issue of what is meant, or should be meant, by the words 'exist' and 'issue of fact' needs some discussion. Also, since things which exist are often said to be *real* I shall also say something briefly about the words 'real' and 'reality'.

I should like to begin by making a point which, so I suspect, has not always been appreciated by professional philosophers: if we depart from the the ordinary usage of a word we are in serious danger of misleading ourselves. This is something which was noted by Berkeley over two centuries ago (note 4.1.). The passage is worth quoting in full:

> *Philonous:* Tell me, Hylas, hath every one a liberty to change the current proper signification annexed to a common name in any language? For example, suppose a traveller should tell you, that in a certain country men might pass unhurt through the fire; and, upon explaining himself, you found he meant by the word *fire* that which others call *water*; or if he should assert that there are trees which walk upon two legs, meaning men by the term trees. Would you think this reasonable?
>
> *Hylas:* No; I should think it absurd. Common custom is the standard of propriety in language.

This is an idea which was later taken up by the philosopher, J.L. Austin, in a particularly forceful way. Austin never claimed that ordinary language was an infallible guide to the nature of reality, but he stressed that if we revise ordinary language we at least need to be clear what it is that we are revising.

One of Austin's memorable examples concerned the word 'real'; and he gives a wealth of examples of ways in which this word is used (note 4.2). Thus to speak of a 'real' oasis implies that what we are looking at is not a mirage; if diamonds are described as 'real' this implies that they are not paste or fake; a 'real' duck is by implication not a toy duck, while if one speaks of the 'real' colour of a woman's hair, this has nothing to do with mirages, fake diamonds, or toys: one is saying that her hair has not been dyed! In general, so Austin argues, it is a mistake to look for some property which all 'real' things have in common. To use his somewhat inelegant expression, it is the word 'unreal' rather than the word 'real' which 'wears the trousers': the function of the word 'real' is to exclude *failure* to be real – and things can fail to be real for a variety of different reasons.

It is also worth noting that the expression 'Do there exist any so-and-sos?' is often equivalent to '*Are there* any so-and-sos?' Thus '*Are there* any dodos?' means the same as 'Do any dodos *exist?*', while '*Are there* any prime numbers between 25 and 30?' means the same as, 'Do any prime numbers between 25 and 30 *exist?*' Although there is a temptation to assume that 'things which exist' are necessarily *solid* items, standard uses of 'exist' do not justify us in thinking in this way. Dodos, when they existed, could properly have been described as 'solid' and it would make sense to speak of *capturing* a few – perhaps in a net. However in the case of prime numbers the idea of capturing them or failing to capture them – whether in a net or by any other means – makes no sense. Similarly, if someone were to ask, 'Are there (or do there exist) any duties which are totally overriding?' then, whatever the answer, there is no expectation that, if the answer is 'yes' one might capture some duties in a net. Similarly we may believe that that there is a virtue in necessity or that there is safety in numbers without being committed to saying that virtue or safety are 'real entities' – a statement to which it does not seem possible to attach any sense.

21

If one discusses the question 'whether God exists' in 'Magnus' terms, one is assimilating it logically – as was pointed out in chapter 1 – to questions such as whether there is a monster in the depths of Loch Ness or whether there are trams in Sheffield. In this context, when people ask whether God exists (or is a 'real existent' or 'genuine reality') one must suppose that the intended contrast is between 'real' and 'illusory' or between 'really existing' and 'existing only in the imagination'. The issue in that case can be described as one of fact. More, however, needs to be said about the circumstances in which we speak of 'facts', since we do so in a variety of different contexts.

In the first place, 'questions of fact' are sometimes contrasted with 'questions of law'. For example the fact may not be in dispute that someone removed a wheelbarrow from my garden last week; however, whether this action constituted burglary is an issue not of fact but of law. Issues of fact can of course be *relevant* to settling issues of law – for example, if it transpired that the accused was nowhere near my garden when the wheelbarrow disappeared then the court would have to bring in a verdict of 'not guilty'. However the pronouncing of the words 'not guilty' is not itself the statement of a further fact but is, as we say, a 'verdict' which is based on the facts which have already been established.

A different contrast is that between 'matters of fact' and 'matters of opinion'. Thus it is a matter of fact that Mozart wrote the serenade, *Eine kleine Nachtmusik,* but it is a matter of opinion whether this composition should rank among his greatest works. Issues of fact may, of course, influence our opinions; for example, in this case a knowledge of some of the musical conventions and practices of Mozart's day might throw light on the originality of this particular piece. However the judgment that it is (or is not) one of his greatest works is not itself the statement of a further fact.

There is also a contrast between fact and interpretation. Thus it might be a fact that a patient in psychotherapy consistently failed to mention, say, his quarrels with his father earlier in his life. If, however, it was then claimed that he had failed to mention them because he found them unpleasant, this would be a matter not of fact but of interpretation. An interpretation, like a judgment of artistic merit, is not simply a further fact.

Finally, – and most importantly for our purposes – a contrast is sometimes drawn between 'fact' and 'myth'. If a statement is one of fact it is said to be 'literally true', whereas a myth, though it may point a moral or be an edifying story, is not a literal record of how things happened.

Trouble lies ahead for us over the word 'myth' because those truths which I have called 'profound truths' (see Chapter 1) are often said to be 'mythical' in character; and this might seem to imply a disparagement or devaluation of profound truth. This is an issue to which I shall return in chapter 7. For the present I am calling attention to the obvious fact that we distinguish between, for instance, Thor, Hercules, centaurs, etc., whom we describe as 'mythical', and, say, Sophocles, Julius Caesar, St. Joan etc. who, as we say, were 'real people'. The distinction between 'real people' and 'pretend people' is of course one that children learn from a very young age.

To elucidate the idea of 'literal' truth I should now like to distinguish those truths which could in principle be picked up by a suitably placed recording device and those which could not. When I say 'could be picked up' I am not talking about what is or is not technologically possible but about what makes logical sense. To return to the examples given earlier, a recording device cannot pick up prime numbers between 25 and 30 or overriding duties – not because the technology is inadequate but because the concepts 'prime number between 25 and 30' and 'overriding duty' are not logically of a kind such that it would make sense to talk in this way: a recording device would neither pick them up nor fail to do so. In contrast, if an episode in, for example, the Trojan war was genuinely historical this implies that such a device, had one been present, would have recorded it. Obviously in the case of events which occurred before the technology for making recording devices existed it would not have been possible in practice to check by this means – any more than it is possible to do so in the case of contemporary events where no recording device is in fact present. Practicalities, however, are irrelevant to the argument: there is no objection in logic to asking what *would* have been found had a recording device been present.

Let us consider how the notion of 'recording device' truth might be applied in legal cases. If a person takes a rake from my shed, this is something which could have been picked up by means of a recording device. However, for logical reasons – and, again, not because of deficient technology – what the device cannot tell us is whether in law the person is guilty of theft. The verdict is not an additional piece of 'recording device' truth; the recording device provides 'the facts' on which a verdict of 'guilty' or 'not guilty' is based.

Similarly there could be recordings of all the various doings of a person, such as Saint Teresa, who spent her life in the service of humanity. If, however, it is then said that she was rightly canonised as a 'saint' this is not a further piece of 'recording device' truth but a judgment based on the recording device truths already available.

In what follows I shall frequently have occasion to ask rhetorically of my readers, 'What *kind* of claim are you making?' In particular I shall be asking whether it is the kind of claim that could be settled by means of a recording device.

If so, then once the recording device has put the facts on record the words in which the claim is expressed are *definitively true*. The word 'definitive' is important here. Thus, if it is claimed that there is a dog in my neighbour's garden, and if a recording device, present at the appropriate place and time, shows both my neighbour's garden and the dog, then by definition that is what 'there is a dog in my neighbour's garden' means. There being a dog in my neighbour's garden just is the combination of events presented on the recording device. In contrast, if all that is picked up by the recording device is my neighbour's garden and some doggy pawmarks and a sound of barking, this may, indeed, give one grounds for thinking it *likely* that there is a dog in my neighbour's garden but the issue is not settled definitively. What is missing is what may be called the 'pay-off' observation – the observation which clinches the matter because it is precisely what 'There is a dog in my neighbour's garden' means or predicts.

It is characteristic of factual statements that they carry predictions of this kind; and if we make would-be factual claims without being able to specify what is predicted then we are misleading ourselves. This is because we are claiming that something is a fact without being prepared to 'back' our claim by indicating what our words mean.

During the rest of the book I shall refer to this argument as the 'verificationist' argument, since it emphases the need to specify how a particular claim is verified (for further discussion of the issues involved see note 4.3).

It follows from the above argument that a distinction is needed between 'supporting evidence' on the one hand and the 'pay-off observation' on the other. Doggy footprints and the sounds of barking are supporting evidence for the statement that there is a dog in my neighbour's garden but they do not make this claim definitively true; if it is to be definitively true there has to be the pay-off observation: that is to say, the recording device must show the dog actually being there.

One final complication requires mention. This concerns the verification of statements which tell us what *generally* happens or what is *liable* to happen. Thus, if someone is described as 'cautious' or 'bad tempered' there are many different ways in which he can show his caution or bad temper. If, for instance, he refuses on a particular occasion to swim in a river on the grounds that the current is stronger than usual, this is supporting evidence for the statement 'he is cautious' but does not settle the matter definitively since the behaviour described may have been uncharacteristic. Similarly if he kicks the cat this provides some degree of supporting evidence that he is bad tempered; but the action may have been atypical or there may have been special reasons for it: to be bad tempered is not just to kick cats but to do any of a variety of things and to do them regularly. 'Cautious' and 'bad tempered' are what Gilbert Ryle has called 'disposition' words (note 4.4). In their case there is a somewhat indefinite list of possible predictions – or, in other words, there are different ways in which one may manifest caution or bad temper. What settles the matter definitively in these cases is not any one specified occurrence but a combination of a sufficient number of occurrences which are relevant. If a person refused ever to drive fast on a motor way, was regularly very restrained in his bidding at bridge, etc. etc., then the point would eventually be reached at which one was entitled to say, 'If that is not being cautious, then I do not know what "being cautious" means'. Similarly if he regularly kicked the cat, responded angrily to the shopkeeper, etc. etc. one would eventually say, 'If that is not being bad tempered then I do not know what "being bad tempered" means'. The important point is that in cases of this kind there may be no *single* pay-off observation as there is if one discovers a dog in one's neighbour's garden, but this does not remove the logical obligation to specify what predictions a would-be factual claim is making.

It follows from all this that factual statements have their own 'logic' and that we are misleading ourselves if we do not take this logic into account. If we claim that God's existence (or non-existence) is an issue of fact we are logically committed to playing a particular language game – that which requires us to specify what is the appropriate 'pay-off' observation. Otherwise we are misleading ourselves with words. This means, in effect, that we end up with what may be called 'the image of the hidden puppeteer' – a being whose existence one claims to *infer* but without any specification of the 'pay-off' observation that would make the claim definitively true. As will be shown in chapter 6, this is one of the central difficulties to which acceptance of the Magnus image gives rise.

CHAPTER 5

The trivialisation of religious issues

IN A WELL-KNOWN PASSAGE Anselm speaks of God as 'that than which greater cannot be thought' (note 5.1). It was also recognised by Aquinas that when the word 'exist' is used of God then (at the very least) some kind of qualification is needed. The following passage illustrates this point:

> We cannot know what God is, but only what he is not. We must therefore consider the ways in which God does not exist, rather than the ways in which he does... The ways in which God does not exist will become apparent if we rule out from him everything inappropriate, such as compositeness, change, and the like (note 5.2)

Surprisingly, however, these reservations are largely lacking among many present day thinkers. For them the question whether God exists is assumed to be a *hypothesis.*

I have no wish to be polemical. However, if only to illustrate that the above assumption is widespread, it is perhaps justified to refer to certain individuals by name.

I start with a quotation from Wallace Matson. I do not know what Matson's religious beliefs are, but I should like to suggest that, as a philosopher, he has 'got it wrong'. He writes as follows:

> The purpose of this book is to investigate the reasonableness of believing that there is at least one god...I shall try to conduct this investigation dispassionately and judiciously, as if we were arguing about the existence of the Himalayan Snowman, or the antineutrino (note 5.3).

Since the issue is presented as being one of fact it is clearly quite proper that one should approach the matter 'dispassionately and judiciously'. I also believe Matson to be right in pointing out, as he does a few lines later, that there is no inconsistency in trying to examine facts dispassionately while nevertheless caring very much about the outcome. In his words:

> Religion is not an intellectual system, but a general orientation to things, a way of life...People do not care about the Snowman and the antineutrino the way they care about God...(note 5.4).

However, there is a further passage which runs as follows:

> There is another important respect in which the question of the existence of God is unlike that of the existence of the Snowman and the antineutrino. In the latter cases, the evidence is not all in; however we know what kind of evidence would be conclusive if found. The reverse is true in natural theology. Here it is safe to say that the evidence is all in. Nobody is likely to turn up some new facts that would drastically strengthen or weaken *the theistic hypothesis* (my italics) (note 5.5).

Whether God exists, then, according to Matson, is a hypothesis which is open to review by evidence, but evidence over and above what we have already is unlikely to be forthcoming.

Richard Swinburne takes a similar view:

> I take the proposition 'God exists' (and the equivalent proposition 'There is a God') to be logically equivalent to 'there exists a person without a body (i.e. a spirit) who is eternal...(note 5.6)

In a later chapter (chapter 14) Swinburne discusses 'the balance of probability'. What is taken for granted, of course, is that it makes sense to speak of God's existence as something which can be probable or improbable. The conclusion that God's existence is probable is also argued for by Montefiore (note 5.7).

The following story has been told of the philosopher, Bertrand Russell. Knowing Russell's professions of atheism someone asked

28

him, What would you say if, after death, you found yourself being ushered through the pearly gates into the presence of God?' Russell thought for a moment, and then replied: 'I would say, "Lord, why didn't you give us more evidence?"'. This anecdote reveals that for Russell, as for many others, the issue of whether God does or does not exist is a factual matter which depends on the correct interpretation of the evidence.

There has recently been a debate between Smart and Haldane (note 5.8), with Smart defending an 'atheist' position and Haldane, a Roman Catholic, defending a 'theist' position. The debate is conducted with the utmost courtesy, but if the arguments in this book are right both parties to this alleged dispute are mistaken. In an introduction written jointly by both authors we read:

> For the most part (our) debate revolves around a familiar set of questions: is there reason to believe in the existence of God? are there grounds to deny that such a thing exists? is theism coherent?

What one misses, however, is any discussion of what, in this context, is actually meant by the word 'exist' (compare chapter 4 of this book) or any recognition that the language of religious commitment has necessarily to be the language of profound truth. It is hard to see how the kind of philosophical discussions which occur in this book can belong elsewhere than in the language of standard truth (note 5.9).

There has also been a recent challenge from Keith Ward to the allegedly 'atheistic' and 'materialistic' assumptions of some of his scientific colleagues, in particular Richard Dawkins and Peter Atkins. Ward's claim, in opposition to theirs, is that:

> a theistic interpretation of evolution and of the findings of the natural sciences is by far the most reasonable... and that it is the *postulate* of God, with its corollary of objective purpose and value, that can best provide an explanation for why the universe is as it is (note 5.10. Italics are mine)

Ward, then, is looking for an 'interpretation of evolution and the findings of the natural sciences', and for him God is a 'postulate' which best makes sense of the phenomena to be explained. This, however, is to play the same 'language game' as that of any biologist or physicist, when in my view he would have done better to insist that the language of profound truth involves a different 'language game'. It seems that even as eminent a scholar as Keith Ward has not completely shaken himself clear of the insidious influence of the 'Magnus' image (note 5.11).

Even the participants in these debates would probably agree that the results are inconclusive. One is tempted to ask whether the question 'Does God exist?' will still be being debated in this same form a thousand years from now, with the same lack of agreement as to its answer. If so, are there not grounds for suspecting that a wrong question has been asked (note 5.12)?

There was a cartoon many years ago in the magazine, *Punch*. The picture was of the outside of a village hall, and all over it were 'bubbles' (representing the speech of those inside the building). These 'bubbles' contained only the juxtaposed words, 'It be', 'It b'aint', 'It be', 'It b'aint' many times over. The caption below said, 'Do come in, Mr.... The debating society is in fine fettle to-night'. I see a mischievous parallel: if the issue of 'theism' versus 'atheism' continues to be debated in terms of which 'side' has got the facts right then there is no way in which the discussion can rise above this level!

My suggstion is that this apparently insoluble dispute has arisen because the issues have mistakenly been couched in 'Magnus' terms. In place of the question 'Does God exist?' we need to substitute the question, What sort of a thing should religious commitment be?

There is a story told of a famous theologian (I do not know if it is true), who was approached by a student claiming that he 'did not believe in God'. The theologian therefore brought out a whole battery of learned arguments designed to show that the student was wrong. The student listened carefully and then said: 'Yes, you have convinced me. Now I believe in God'. It was said that the theologian was horrified, saying afterwards, 'Whatever I had done I certainly had not converted him to the kind of God I believe in'. Certainly, as the story is told, there is no evidence that the student underwent a change of heart or made any commitment to live his life in a new way.

The important point, as I see it, is that if 'the existence of God' is discussed in 'Magnus' terms this has nothing to do with religious commitment. Thus if one decided that, *as a matter of fact*, God existed and if as a result one made certain changes in one's life, one would indeed be adapting to the facts as one understood them, but this would be no more than a policy of prudence which could justifiably be modified if one later decided that the facts were different.

What I want to offer at this point may be called a 'stipulative' definition of religious commitment – that is, a proposal or recommendation that the expression 'religious commitment' be understood in a particular way (note 5.13). My stipulation is that no commitment should count as 'religious' unless it is unconditional – that is, unless one holds to it whatever the facts turn out to be.

An example of a commitment that would qualify as being 'religious' in this sense is that made by Job. The facts – what God did to him – were irrelevant: he responded, 'Though he slay me, yet will I trust in him' (note 5.14); and we are to infer that he would have gone on saying this whatever misfortunes God or Satan imposed on him. By all rights, given that people receive their deserts, he might have expected to have been successful and prosperous. Yet in fact he was afflicted by calamity after calamity. His response is on the present definition a religious one. If someone had asked what were the *conditions* in which he would have been willing to 'curse God and die' (note 5.15) it is clear from the story that there would have been none. This is what is meant by saying his commitment was 'unconditional' (note 5.16).

To some people marriage is a religious commitment in this sense. This is the case if it is undertaken 'for better or for worse' (note 5.17), with the intention that the partnership cannot be dissolved merely because the going may sometimes get hard.

If God existed in a literal sense it is hard to see how any commitment to him could be other than conditional. It might arguably be wise policy to follow certain ritualistic observances, but wise policy is not the same as religious commitment. At one point Don

Cupitt has mischievously quoted the words of a hymn which seemingly fails to distinguish between the two:

> Whatever, Lord, we give to Thee
> Repaid a thousandfold will be;
> Then gladly will we give to thee,
> Who givest all (note 5.18).

He then adds:

> Imagine that the hymn-writer is meditating upon the soundness of an investment and say that verse with emphasis on the word 'gladly', and the absurdity will become apparent.

Now there is a powerful strand in the Christian tradition – it will be discussed further in chapter 7 – by which one can say, not what God is, but only what he is not (note 5.19). The important insight here, it seems to me, is that any other view is degrading to religion. In the last resort one can only be silent.

This, I suggest, is why all thinking in 'Magnus' terms has to be inadequate. Magnus has been caricatured as a being who, if he exists at all, exists in an entirely literal sense. However if we think in this way we are failing to do justice to God's ineffability (and even the word 'ineffable' is of course itself inadequate).

My next move must therefore be to emphasise further the dangers of literalness. To make my point I shall adopt the technique of trying to win the reader over by small stages – beginning with statements which no one will dispute and then drawing out the consequences. Basically, one starts where the other person is and tries to see things from their point of view rather than forcing on them something which may seem controversial and provocative (note 5.20).

Now I assume without question that any thoughtful person professing belief in God would agree that it is degrading to God to think of him as a bearded figure in the sky. It would be agreed that this is a childish, not to say pagan, idea which sets 'bounds' to God in a wholly inappropriate way.

It would also be agreed that the phrase in the Apostles' creed 'sitteth on the right hand of God the Father, Almighty' should not be taken to imply that God in any literal sense has a right hand.

32

The next stage is to consider language which ascribes emotional states to God. Such language is regularly used of the god of the old testament; for instance he is reported as showing grief ('It repented the Lord that he had made man on the earth, and it grieved him at his heart') (note 5.21). In the Christian era there are again references to God's anger or wrath, as when Marlowe's Faustus exclaims:

Mountains and hills, come, come, and fall on me,
And hide me from the heavy wrath of God (note 5.22).

Moreover both in the old and new testaments and in the Christian era there are many references to God's love (note 5.23).

However, when thoughtful people talk nowadays of God's anger or of God's love, it is safe to say that few of them believe that the words 'anger' and 'love' are to be understood literally. To suppose otherwise would be to trivialise God. In the word's of a well known hymn, God's love is

...perfect love, all human thought transcending
(note 5.24).

It is also common to speak of the 'will' of God. Here, too, it seems absurd to suppose that we have suddenly crossed a boundary from non-literalness to literalness. There may perhaps be a temptation here to feel that a person's 'will' is something more 'spiritual' than their right hand; but it is hard to see how such a view can be consistently maintained.

Next there is the issue of the 'maleness' of God. For historical reasons – in particular because most societies have been male dominated – God is commonly thought of as 'male'; but, in the words of Keith Ward,

few Christians would seriously suppose that God the Father has a physical body, or that God is literally father in the sense of being a male carrier of human genes. Such statements are readily characterised as metaphor (note 5.25).

What seems clear in general is that when we speak of God we have perforce to make use of expressions which we have learned in the course of acquiring language. In childhood we hear others use

33

words and repeat them ourselves – and we are corrected if we use them inappropriately. No word's meaning can be learned in isolation from the social context in which it is used (note 5.26).

However, it seems to me that many present-day thinkers have not followed through non-literalist interpretations of 'God'-language to their logical limits. In the passage just quoted Keith Ward continues:

> But is it any less metaphorical to speak of God as a non-embodied mind? The Church Fathers very rarely speak of God as a cosmic mind (*nous*); and if the physical properties ascribed to God in the Bible should be taken as metaphorical because of God's transcendence of all human images, why should not the mental properties also be taken as metaphorical, because of God's transcendence of all human concepts?
>
> The obvious reply is that God cannot transcend *all human concepts, since then nothing at all could be said of God; not even that God exists* (note 5.27; italics mine)

Ward then goes on to suggest that certain things are true of God in a literal sense, for instance that God knows all things.

But can there be a valid boundary of this kind? If 'right hand', 'anger', 'love', 'will', 'he', and other expressions cannot be used literally of God, why should this not also be true of the central 'ontological' words, 'exist', 'cause', and 'real'? If the literal expressions 'right hand', 'anger', 'love', 'will', and 'he' are degrading to God why should not 'exist', 'cause' and 'real' be equally degrading?

The inference has to be that there is no appropriate response to God other than silence. This is far from being a novel conclusion; however I would suggest that as a result of 'Magnus' ways of thinking it has been allowed to fall into the background.

CHAPTER 6

The image of the hidden puppeteer

IT WAS SUGGESTED in the last chapter that it is *degrading* to God
to argue about his existence as though it were an issue of fact.
In this chapter I shall try to show that to do so is logically muddled
and self-defeating. This I do by referring back to 'the image of the
hidden puppeteer' mentioned in chapter 4.

Within the broad grouping 'scientific language' there are, of
course, many sub-groups. In Wittgenstein's terminology (note
6.1), many different 'language games' are played, each having its
own set of 'rules'. In what follows I shall not focus on technical scientific language – generalisations, mathematical formulae, 'models'
of reality and the like – but on what may be called the language of
common sense and in particular on 'matters of fact' in the sense
described in chapter 4. As Cupitt has pointed out (note 6.2), such
language has to be 'impersonal, dispassionate and value-neutral'.
Before about the 16th century it seems plain that for most language
users no clear distinction existed between expressions designed to
tell us what is the case and expressions whose function, for example, is to persuade, edify, punish, or perform rituals.

The important point about issues of fact is that they have to be
determined by evidence. This point may seem obvious, but its
implications have not always been fully appreciated.

If the question 'whether God exists' is an issue of fact certain
consequences follow. In particular, it is clear that 'exist' is being
applied to him in exactly the same sense as is applicable when one
discusses the existence of trams in Sheffield or the existence of the
Loch Ness monster. However, unless we believe naively in a bearded

figure in the sky we are forced to say that God is different from a tram or from the Loch Ness monster in that he is a 'non-material' being; moreover since he is not part of the order of nature we must say that he is a 'supernatural' being. It is to set the stage for challenging this whole way of thinking that I have, as a caricature, introduced the name 'Magnus'. Magnus is the non-material, supernatural being whose existence or non-existence is an issue of fact.

It was argued in chapter 4 that if a meaningful claim is made on an issue of fact there has to be, at least implicitly, a specification as to how the statement in question can be verified – a specification of what a recording device would have picked up or of what would constitute a decisive 'pay-off' observation. If, however, we assume that the question of whether or not God exists is an issue of fact this is precisely what we find ourselves unable to do.

The point is not that it is *difficult to be sure* whether God exists. There are, of course, plenty of questions of fact where at present we are unsure of the answers, for example whether there are living beings elsewhere in space. What I am saying is that if we present the issue of God's existence in these terms we are misleading ourselves because the standard procedures for determining issues of fact cannot be specified.

What has gone wrong is that we are in bondage to what I call 'the image of the hidden puppeteer'. If we see a puppet on a stage we can make the inference that a puppeteer behind the scenes is pulling the strings. In this case, however, the pay-off observation can be achieved if we walk behind the stage and come face to face with the puppeteer, whereas in the case of God in the 'Magnus' sense (i.e. a supernatural, non-material entity) we are in effect asking about a hidden puppeteer in a context where no specification has been given of what would count as the pay-off observation. If God were thought of as a person with a beard who lived beyond the clouds there would at least be no problem of logic or method: one would organise a space expedition and try to find him. Acquiring appropriate evidence might be difficult but at least there would be no dispute over the kind of evidence that would settle the matter. It is commonly agreed, however, that people have outgrown the idea of a bearded figure who lives in the sky and that we need

36

instead to think of him rather as a 'spiritual' being, or perhaps as a 'pure intelligence' or 'creative mind' (note 6.3). Since, however, this implies a being that cannot be touched or seen we have thereby deprived ourselves of the possibility of specifying what would count as the pay-off observation.

To illustrate this point further it may be helpful to consider arguments about the lay-out of the monument at Stonehenge or that of the Great Pyramid. There may seemingly be signs of 'purposefulness' about the ways in which the stones are arranged which suggest considerable knowledge of astronomy on the part of the designers; and there can be legitimate discussion as to how much knowledge they in fact possessed. The important point here, however, is that there could in principle have been a pay-off observation: an observer or a recording device could have shown people discussing astronomy in appropriate terms. In contrast, to argue whether 'the universe' shows similar signs of 'planning' is a useless hypothesis unless there is some indication of what the observer or the recording device is supposed to be picking up.

It is, of course, possible to recognise systems and patterns; this is something which we do the whole time. Some things are ordered, whilst some are chaotic; and in standard cases it is not difficult to tell the difference between the two. Moreover it is not obviously absurd to say that the universe is a 'cosmos' or is like a well-kept garden rather than like a wilderness (note 6.4). None of this, however, leads to the idea of an independently observable designer.

Now it may be objected that if God is a 'spiritual' and 'incorporeal' being the need for a pay-off observation cannot apply. Observers and recording devices, it might be said, can pick up only *material* entities; our sense organs are so made that they respond only when something *physical* is present. To expect to 'observe' God in this way is to be tied to 'materialist' assumptions when the whole question at issue is whether there are non-material or spiritual entities in addition.

If people argue in this way, however, the onus is on them to specify what kind of a thing a non-material entity could be. How does one recognise it? What distinction is being marked in this context between the 'material' and the 'non-material'?

One might perhaps go to the literal meaning of the word 'spirit' – that is, 'wind' or 'breath'. One can feel the pressure of the wind even though there is nothing to be seen, and the idea of a force such as the wind is of course intelligible. If, however, the only evidence for such forces is what are thought to be their effects we are again in the position of not having a pay-off observation. It is not false, but simply pointless, to postulate an unobservable 'cause' when the only available evidence consists of its alleged 'effects'.

We can also imagine ourselves carrying out what are called 'acts of will'. Thus if I decide to raise my arm I find – unless I am paralysed – that I am able to do so. It is quite unnecessary, however, to say that in this kind of situation there has been an unobservable 'mental' or 'spiritual' occurrence which has then acted causally on the 'physical' world. This is the language of Cartesian dualism (see Chapter 3); but there is no valid justification for supposing that this kind of 'dualist' approach is somehow more 'religious' than the approach of those who call themselves 'behaviourists', 'anti-dualists', and the like.

There is also the objection that the above argument is nothing more than a kind of linguistic sleight of hand. If one defines one's terms in a particular way, so it might be argued, then of course – as a matter of logic – certain conclusions follow. The crucial issue, however, on this view is whether the definitions were correct in the first place. In the present case may it not be that by choosing to define the words 'exist' and 'fact' in a particular way one is begging the important question? The objector might then say that the proposal simply reflects a narrow-minded form of materialism that need be binding on no one.

However it is not the case that the word 'exist' has been arbitrarily defined. As has already been made clear, standard usage is the relevant criterion (see the start of chapter 4 and the quotation from Berkeley); and in that case it is for those who want to innovate to give reasons for doing so. Those who claim that '"Spiritual entities exist as well as material ones" is an issue of fact' are innovating with the words 'exist' and 'fact' and failing to make clear what kind of 'fact' is involved. We are often told that there is merit in open-mindedness, which indeed there is. It does not follow, however, that there is merit in muddle-headedness! To profess to believe – as an issue of fact – that a non-material God exists is wrong not because it is mistaken and must therefore give place to atheism but because it involves using language in a muddled and self-defeating way.

In subsequent chapters I shall refer to this group of difficulties as the 'verificationist' difficulties. In brief, if one treats the question, 'Does God exist?' as an issue of fact, not only is this degrading to religion, as argued in chapter 5; there is the further objection that one is failing to follow the logical rules which the making of factual claims requires.

CHAPTER 7

Mythoi and the way of silence

I F TALK OF GOD – and, indeed, religious language in general – is not to be taken literally one may be tempted to say that it is the language of myth or parable or that it expresses 'poetic truth'. There are some for whom this point is obvious and presents no difficulty; however there may be others who feel that expressions such as 'myth', 'parable', and 'poetic truth' *take something away.*

One can sympathise with this. When we say, for example, that accounts of the doings of Zeus, Wotan, etc. are 'myths' this implies that no such beings as Zeus or Wotan ever existed. For those still trapped in 'Magnus' ways of thinking one is therefore rubbing salt into the wound: they will suppose that what is being said that God no more exists than does Zeus or Wotan: he is a 'mere' myth – a poetic fiction. Even if it is pointed out that myths can convey an important message, the impression may still be given that those who say that religious truths are the language of myth do not *really* believe them or at best are somewhat half-hearted in their beliefs (note 7.1). One can also imagine the religious sceptic sneering at those who for good enough reasons find traditional beliefs untenable but who then take refuge in saying that these beliefs should be reinterpreted as 'myths'.

The position has been brilliantly satirised in Chapter 8 of *Yes, Prime Minister: The Diaries of the Right Hon. James Hacker* (note 7.2). Here are some sample passages:

> Peter told me that Mike is a modernist... 'A theological term, Prime Minister. It seems that he accepts that some of the events described in the Bible are not *literally* true

40

– he sees them as metaphors, legends or myths. He is interested in the spiritual and philosophical truth behind the stories'.

Later Sir Humphrey says to Hacker:

'In the Church of England the word Modernist is code for non-believer'. 'An atheist?' I asked with surprise. 'Oh no, Prime Minister', he replied wickedly. 'An atheist clergyman couldn't continue to draw his stipend. So when they stop believing in God they call themselves modernists'.

Although this is satire, the authors of *Yes, Prime Minister* have raised a point which to some people causes serious concern. This can be shown by the controversy which arose when a group of theologians published a seemingly innocent book entitled *The Myth of God Incarnate* (note 7.3). It was immediately clear that some people objected to the word 'myth', and soon afterwards there was a counterblast in the form of a book entitled *The Truth of God Incarnate* (note 7.4); and other books followed (note 7.5).

At an earlier date Richard Braithwaite had written a booklet entitled *An Empiricist's View of the Nature of Religious Belief* (note 7.6) in which he described religious beliefs as 'stories', though allowing that the words 'parable', 'fairy story', 'allegory', 'fable', 'tale' and 'myth' would also have served his purpose. Braithwaite claimed that people were helped in their behaviour by these stories even though 'the story associated with the behaviour policy is not believed' (note 7.7).

Braithwaite's view is tantamount to a rejection of the Magnus image (note 7.8). However it is arguable that in using the word 'empiricist' and in failing to allay possible worries over the use of the word 'story' he was being unnecessarily provocative. 'Empiricism', as the term is normally understood, is basically the claim that 'empirical' statements – those based on experience and observation – have some kind of privileged status or refer to 'what really exists'. However, it is not clear what 'really exists' could mean in this context: as was shown at the start of chapter 4, there are some perfectly proper statements containing the word 'exist' which are not based on experience and observation, such as 'Do there exist any prime numbers between twenty five and thirty?' or 'Do there exist any duties which are totally overriding?' The present book can, in a sense, be regarded as an *attack* on empiricism, since it is a plea that empirical statements – which on my view are a sub-group of 'standard' truths – should not be overvalued at the expense of 'profound' truths. Braithwaite also seems to be claiming that these stories help people in their behaviour, but whether they do so is clearly an issue of fact, in which case the idea of *unconditional* commitment is missing. I myself, in an earlier book (note 7.9) put forward a view similar to Braithwaite in that I suggested that religious language was essentially the language of parable; and, although I still believe that in an important sense this is correct, the main reason why I now wish to modify it is that use of the word 'parable' is open to misunderstanding.

It was to forestall any such misunderstandings over the words 'myth', 'parable', 'story', etc. that I drew the distinction in Chapter 1 between *standard truth* and *profound truth*. It was intended as a deliberate challenge to any present day thinker who claims that we should offer more respect to literal ('factual') truth than to poetic truth. It is more appropriate, surely, to say that these ways of using language are *different*, not that one kind of 'language game' is 'better' than another. In accordance with this objective my present purpose is to find a way of characterising religious language which will cause fewest misunderstandings.

After hesitation I have decided to make use of what is in effect a technical word which I am then free to define in my own way. This word is *mythos* (plural *mythoi*). It is the Greek original from which the English word 'myth' is derived; and my intention is that some, but not all, of the associations with the word 'myth' be retained.

I should like to make the following stipulations:

(i) a mythos must convey some kind of profound truth

(ii) historical and scientific issues (whether certain events actually happened as recorded in the myth) are irrelevant

(iii) some mythoi are more powerful – more insightful – than others or convey a more important message.

Because mythoi are by definition expressions of profound truth any suggestion of disparagement ('*merely* a myth') is ruled out.

I should like to give two examples. In the first place, the doctrine of the 'social contract' can properly be described as a mythos. The suggestion is that human beings met together and chose to put themselves under the rule of law, since the alternative would be anarchy. In the words of Hobbes there would be

> no arts; no letters; no society; and which is worst of all, continual fear and danger of violent death; and the life of man, solitary, poor, nasty, brutish and short (note 7.10).

Rousseau's *Social Contract* also treats of the same theme.

> Man is born free; and everywhere he is in chains... How did this change come about? I do not know. What can make it legitimate? That question I think I can answer (note 7.11).

It is not necessary to believe, as a matter of literal historical truth, that human beings at a particular occasion in time chose to band together and sign an agreement for their mutual protection. The idea of a social contract is a mythos: it calls attention to the profound truth (if it is one) that we are *implicitly* under contract to obey the law; only if such a contract exists can law enforcement by the state be justified.

In this case the three criteria for 'mythos' are satisfied. In the first place profound truths are at stake, since the doctrine is relevant to the relationships of human beings living in society. Secondly, the question of whether as a matter of history our ancestors at some point banded together to sign a written contract is irrelevant. Thirdly, the insights derived from this doctrine are adjudged by many to be powerful and important ones.

My second example of a mythos is the story of Adam and Eve in the garden of Eden (note 7.12). This mythos makes sense, of course, only if conjoined with a group of other mythoi: these mythoi remind us of our human pride and folly and of our tendency to choose evil rather than good; they then point to the need for a redeemer – a second Adam – who will make it possible for fallen man to be restored to a new relationship with God. In this case, too, the three criteria for 'mythos' are satisfied. Thus the language is that of profound truth; the historical accuracy of what is described

43

is arguably unimportant, and the religious insights may for some people be very powerful.

It is not the purpose of this book to *commend* any particular mythoi; this is a matter of individual choice for the reader. However I hope I have explicated the notion of 'mythos' in a way which leads to increased understanding of what religious language should aim to achieve.

It remains for me to make some comments about 'apophatic' (or 'negative') theology and about the way of silence (note 7.13).

One of the important insights which will be found in many different religious traditions is that any language in which we try to speak of the sacred is inadequate. In the Old Testament an important characteristic of Jehovah was his holiness – his name was too sacred to mention. Even at the present time there is still the practice of writing 'G-d' in place of 'God', which is a similar form of reverence. In other parts of the world one can find the same message. Thus according to H.D. Lewis (note 7.14) there is an Indian text in the writings of the commentator, Samkara, which

> tells of a pupil who pleads with his teacher to expound to him the nature of the Absolute Self understood religiously as Brahman. To each request the teacher turns a deaf ear until at last he answers the insistent 'Teach me, Sir' with the words 'I am teaching you but you do not follow; the Self is silence'.

I should now like to present a series of quotations from pre-16th century Christian thinkers which illustrate that many of them were well aware that the question, 'Does God exist?' is by no means a straightforward one and that religious commitment does not necessarily require an unqualified affirmative answer.

Particularly striking is the following passage from Scotus Erigena:

> When it is said that God *wills, loves, cares for, sees, hears,* and the like, we must suppose that his ineffable essence and goodness are being conveyed to us in human terms, lest our true and devoted Christian faith should so far be silent about the Creator of all things as not to dare to say anything of him at all (note 7.15).

44

The following passages are the work of an unknown author who took over the name of Dionysius the Areopagite, St. Paul's chief convert at Athens (note 7.16). He is commonly referred to as the 'Pseudo-Dionysius'. Here is the first:

> My argument now rises from what is below up to the transcendent, and the more it climbs, the more language falters, and when it jas passed up and beyond the ascent, it will turn silent completely, since it will finally be at one with him who is indescribable' (note 7.17).

Here is the second:

> It is beyond assertion and denial. We make assertions and denials of what is next to it, but never of it, for it is both beyond every assertion, being the perfect and unique cause of all things, and, by virtue of its preeminently simple and absolute nature, free of every limitation, beyond every limitation; it is also beyond every denial (note 7.18).

Here is the third:

> He is described as invisible, infinite, ungraspable, and other things which show not what he is but what in fact he is not. This second way of talking about him seems to me much more appropriate, for .... God is in no way like the things that have being and we have no knowledge at all of his incomprehensible and ineffable transcendence and invisibility (note 7.19).

My next quotation is from Meister Eckhart

> Everything in the Godhead is one, and of that there is nothing to be said (note 7.20).

I should also like to quote a remarkable passage from St. Nicholas of Cusa:

> Keep in mind that in this world we walk in the way of metaphor and enigmatic images because the spirit of truth is not of this world and can be grasped by us only in so far as metaphors and symbols, which we recognise as such, carry us onward to that which is not known (note 7.21).

45

The following passage from Jacob Boehme is one which includes the word 'supernatural'. However it seems plain that in this passage the overtones which modern thinking gives to the word are lacking:

> That which is finite cannot conceive of the infinite; that which hath a beginning cannot conceive of that which is without beginning and without end.... Likewise we cannot conceive of that which exists eternally in God... in any other way than by speaking of them as though they had a beginning in time... (p.59) I advise the reader, whenever I am speaking of the Godhead and its great mystery, not to conceive of what I say as if it were to be understood in a terrestrial sense, but to regard it from a higher point of view in a supernatural aspect. (note 7.22).

Many years ago I read somewhere (I do not remember the source) that it would be better to symbolise God as a worm rather than as a person, since in that case no one would be tempted to mistake the symbol for the original.

A central theme in many of the above passages is that, in all strictness, nothing can be said of God. The appropriate response must therefore be one of silence.

By implication, however, this has to be a *reverent* silence – the silence of what has been called 'the deeply kneeling man' (note 7.23). Mythoi are not just edifying stories.

Once the need for silence is accepted, we will not be misleading ourselves if we qualify, or modify, this silence by the telling of mythoi. In these mythoi we have no option but to use words drawn from human experience, for example 'father', 'shepherd', 'love', 'light', and many others. I am saying nothing in the least original when I insist that such language should not be taken literally. I have, however, tried to press this point to its logical conclusion by insisting that the expressions 'is real', 'exists', and 'causes things to happen' should not be taken literally either.

In the chapters which follow I shall try to exhibit some of the differences between the interpretation of religious language in 'Magnus' (literal) terms and its interpretation in terms of mythoi.

CHAPTER 8

Prayer in 'Magnus' terms

THIS CHAPTER AND the next two will follow the same format. I shall first try to exhibit the absurdities which arise from 'Magnus' ways of thinking, and I shall then argue that if we wish to make a commitment which genuinely counts as 'religious' we need to turn instead to profound language and the way of silence. The present chapter is concerned with prayer, chapter 9 with miracles, and chapter 10 with various issues of Christian doctrine.

If we think of prayer in 'Magnus' terms this implies that *there is someone there* to whom we are praying. The words 'there is' have to be taken literally, even though the word 'there' cannot be interpreted spatially. If prayer is thought of in this way it may be (though it need not be) *petitionary* prayer – a request to a supernatural being to interfere in the course of nature and do things which he would otherwise not have done.

I shall argue that this view of prayer is untenable for three reasons, which I shall label the 'necessity for statistics argument', the 'verification argument', and the 'moral argument'.

(i) *The necessity for statistics argument.*

If we think of prayer in 'Magnus' terms the question immediately arises as to whether prayers have any effect. This is clearly an issue of fact.

Now, as has already been pointed out, issues of fact are outside the scope of this book: on such issues readers must make up their own minds in the light of the best evidence available. My purpose in the present section of this chapter is to *draw out the logical consequences* of supposing the issue to be one of fact. I shall try to show that these consequences are unacceptable. From this it follows that thinking of prayer in 'Magnus' terms – that is, in terms of requesting a supernatural being to exert his supernatural power – is unacceptable also.

The first point to note is that if the issue is one of fact then the best way of obtaining information is to use what can broadly be called 'scientific method'. Scientific method can take on a variety of different forms, but one of its central characteristics – provided the context is appropriate – is a willingness, to carry out comparisons by means of statistics.

I say 'provided the context is appropriate' because the application of statistical methods to determine issues of fact is sometimes unnecessary. For example, I can be sure without any statistics that if I let go of a book then it will fall to the ground. The important point, however, is that even here I am implicitly making use of statistical methods, since I have had many past experiences unsupported bodies and in all cases the positive results (falling) have been legion and the negative results (not falling) have been zero. If something is totally obvious one stops counting instances!

Some people may feel that an exception needs to be made if one is studying human relationships. Humans, it might be said, have free choice, and if, for instance, I know that someone is making me the object of a statistical comparison I can quite well choose to be 'bolshie' and behave in uncharacteristic fashion! This does, indeed, prove that the ways in which people view a situation and how they verbalise about it may influence their behaviour. However, even in the field of human relations, when we make judgments about people, we are implicitly relying on statistics. It is true that I can know my friend to be trustworthy without any systematic counting of the instances in which he has let me down and compared them with the number of instances when he has not let me down; but as a point of logic I cannot say he is trustworthy unless the count of the former is zero. The choice is not between statistics and no statistics but between using statistics correctly so as to obtain helpful information and using them incorrectly so that one ends up with useless or misleading information. In it is not enough to

48

rely on so-called 'anecdotal' evidence, that is, accounts of events which allegedly happened but at no clearly specified time and with no corroborative details. Anecdotes can form the starting point for more systematic enquiry but they cannot on their own tell us how often an event of a particular kind occurs and do not therefore allow the kind of generalisation which is essential for scientific understanding. Moreover it is easy to mislead oneself by assuming that because a particular event was *followed by* another event the first was necessarily the cause of the second.

Now there may be those who say that collecting statistics about the efficacy of prayer is as unnecessary as collecting statistics about falling bodies. This is because they regard it as obvious that prayers have no effect. Prayers for rain, they would say, have no effect on the weather and prayers for the mending of a broken down motor vehicle are less effective than securing the services of a knowledgeable mechanic (note 8.1).

Others might argue, however, that such evidence is inconclusive. For instance it might be said that a genuinely Christian prayer is one that must be asked 'in Jesus' name'; the fact, therefore, that poorly prepared or selfish prayers are sometimes unanswered does not prove that prayers are *never* answered (note 8.2).

I should like to suggest that disputes along these lines are similar to those which have been discussed earlier in the book in connection with 'the existence of God' (see chapter 5). There is assertion and counter-assertion but little or no prospect of one side persuading the other to think differently. The existence of this deadlock suggests that we should consider carefully whether there is something wrong with the question being asked. I shall argue in section (iii) of this chapter that the question, 'Does God *in fact* answer prayer?' represents a misunderstanding of what prayer should be. For the present, however, I shall continue to draw out the logical consequences of posing the question in this way.

If the issue is genuinely one of fact then, arguably, it is surprising that agreement on the answer has not been reached many decades ago. It is true that there are some issues of fact where the evidence is still inconclusive; for example we do not know for certain whether there is life on Mars. In these cases, however, what is needed is better research techniques. In contrast, if the question is whether prayer is effective, the research techniques already exist: one might, for instance, design a medical experiment in which one group of patients received standard treatment plus prayer and a control group of suitably matched patients received standard treatment on its own. There would of course be problems of 'matching', and to control for the influence of all relevant factors would by no means be easy (see below); nevertheless there is no reason in principle why a valid experiment should not be carried out; and if the initial experiments were inconclusive more refined techniques could then be introduced.

In point of fact statistics have already been used to test the efficacy of prayer (see Francis Galton's book *Inquiries into Human Faculty and Its Development*, published in 1883 (note 8.3). During the course of his discussion Galton presents a statistical table showing that 97 members of royal houses, all of whom were regularly prayed for in public, enjoyed on average no greater longevity than various groups of professionals not so prayed for. He concludes:

> The prayer has therefore no efficacy, unless the very questionable hypothesis be raised, that the conditions of royal life may naturally be yet more fatal, and that their influence is partly, though incompletely, neutralised by the effect of public prayers (op.cit. p.282).

Later he writes:

> If prayerful habits had influence on emporal success, it is very probable... that insurance offices ... would long ago have discovered and made allowance for it. It would be most unwise, from a business point of view, to allow the devout, supposing their greater longevity even probable, to obtain annuities at the same low rates as the profane ... Insurance offices, so wakeful to sanatory influences, absolutely ignore prayer as one of them... How is it possible to explain why the Quakers, who are most devout and most shrewd men of business, have ignored these considerations, except on the grounds that they do not really believe in what they and others freely assert about the efficacy of prayer (ibid. pp.292-3)

A critical but sympathetic examination of Galton's arguments will be found in Brummer (see again note 8.2).

Now no one would dispute that in an experiment on the effectiveness of prayer all kinds of complex factors may be at work. For example a drug may have beneficial effects not because of its chemical properties but because the recipient *believes* it will work (something which is referred to as a 'placebo' effect). There can also be so-called 'Hawthorne' effects – where the very feeling that something is being done, no matter what – may promote recovery, while it is commonly agreed among some psychotherapists that the so-called 'transference situation' – that is, the relationship between therapist and patient – may in some circumstances be used to very positive effect. There may also be situations where healing effects may be due to what some doctors call 'tender loving care' (TLC). Exactly how TLC might work is a matter for debate, but one possibility is that it leads to greater relaxation on the part of the patient and thus provides a better opportunity for the natural healing processes of the body to have some effect. Moreover if what at present are regarded, rightly or wrongly, as 'unorthodox' methods turn out to be beneficial – for instance acupuncture, hypnotherapy, or herbal therapy, – then in due course these methods will figure more prominently in medical textbooks. There is no substitute for systematic investigation of the facts.

Moreover, if we think of prayer in 'Magnus' terms it would make sense for the government of a particular country to fund research into its medical effectiveness. Applications for grants would be considered along with competing applications, and financial support would be given (as already happens) to those research proposals which in the opinion of specialist advisers had the best prospects for success. If such applications are not currently being received this is presumably because everyone knows that they would have no chance of success – the only alternative being to suppose that the medical establishment as a whole are so blinkered in their outlook that they are unwilling to consider novel but unconventional treatments!

Some may be tempted to argue that prayer works by 'auto-suggestion'. In 'Magnus' terms this means that if a person feels spiritually renewed after praying this is not because a supernatural being

51

brought about the renewal but because of their own belief that their condition was improving. Prayer, on this showing, is a way of 'geeing oneself up'. These, however, are not alternative explanations of the efficacy of prayer, since, as was shown in chapter 6, the first alternative – intervention by Magnus – is not an explanation at all but the product of logical confusion. Whether going through the motions of 'geeing oneself up' is a helpful thing to do is an issue of fact and therefore outside the scope of the present enquiry.

Whatever turns out to be the case, my central point is that even if prayers for recovery from sickness turned out to be effective there would still be nothing religious about them in the sense given to the word 'religious' in this book.

This point should perhaps be discussed further. 'Magnus' has been defined as a 'non-physical' being, which carries the implication that he might be willing to work by 'non-physical' methods (whatever this might mean). There may therefore be a temptation to suppose that God has a special interest not just in conventional medicine, which is assumed to be 'materialist' in its approach, but also in more unorthodox forms of treatment such as those mentioned above – acupuncture, hypnotherapy, or herbal therapy. These treatments can quite properly, in the present state of knowledge, be referred to as 'alternative medicine', but nothing at all is gained by calling them 'non-material'. Even if the dichotomy into 'material' and 'non-material' had been a useful one those who use it would still have to say that acupuncture was a 'material' form of treatment, and though they might wish to say that hypnotherapy works on 'the mind' it is more appropriate to say that hypnotherapists use verbal stimuli to help their patients respond in particular ways. To suppose that there is something more 'devout' or 'religious' about the use of alternative medicine is to confuse standard truth with profound truth. The same is true, incidentally, of so-called 'paranormal' phenomena – telepathy, precognition, clairvoyance, psychokinesis, and the like. As I have argued elsewhere (note 8.4), to suppose that such phenomena, if they exist, would provide some sort of a buttress for a religious view of the world must surely be mistaken. Such are the confusions which the idea of a 'non-material' God can generate.

In sum, if we think of prayer in 'Magnus' terms we are logically committed to supposing that scientific research methods are the way to determine the appropriatenesss of prayer. They can, indeed, determine whether praying is *effective*, but from a religious point of view this is not what one should be looking for.

(ii) *The verificationist argument*

There are further difficulties if we think of prayer in 'Magnus' terms – the so-called verificationist difficulties mentioned in chapter 6. Again there is no need for present purposes to take sides on any issue of fact; rather; the relevant question is, 'If the facts turned out to be of a certain kind what would we be entitled to say?'

Let us therefore assume, for purposes of argument, that prayers for rain are in fact regularly followed by rain or – if a more edifying example is preferred – that prayers for recovery from sickness, made in a spirit of unselfishness, are sometimes followed by such recovery. If we think in 'Magnus' terms we would have to say that the successful outcomes are the result of activity on the part of a supernatural being. To talk in this way, however, without specifying what would *count* as a case of 'activity on the part of a supernatural being' is to mislead ourselves with words. If a human being shuts a door one could in principle watch them doing so, but how could one watch a supernatural being at work? It is hard to see what meaning can be given to the claim that the door shut 'because a supernatural being caused it to do so'.

Someone might argue that invisible agencies can sometimes be operative, but, again, what can this mean? It is a matter of familiar experience that the wind sometimes causes doors to shut, and we can imagine a situation where a door blew shut at the most timely moment, which might suggest benevolent planning by an invisible agent. However, in the situation which I am describing one can feel the wind even though one cannot see it, and it is not therefore misleading to ascribe causal powers to the wind. Unless, however, one thinks of a god with a tangible body there can as a matter of logic be no justification for saying in any literal sense that it was an act of God which caused the door to shut. Similarly, if prayers for rain are followed by rain, there is nothing in that situation which would entitle us to say, 'God brought this about'. We would be justified in concluding only that some unknown force was influencing the weather. Whatever in fact happened there would be no grounds for saying that the events in question were 'due to the activity of God'.

(iii) *The moral argument*

If we think of prayer in 'Magnus' terms what we are envisaging is a situation in which God intervenes to restore someone's health *when he would not otherwise have done so.* This raises the question of what sort of a God it could be who brings about the recovery of someone just because she was lucky enough to have friends or relatives praying for her. In this connection I cannot do better than quote the words of Helen Oppenheimer (note 8.5)

> What is hard to believe in is a God who is supposed to withold his favour from some apparently worthy person or cause for whom nobody has happened to intercede

The idea that any of us should have the power to persuade God to intervene in this way is surely immoral in itself; and it is doubly immoral if the assumption is made that those not so prayed for will have less chance of recovery.

In view of the above arguments, what is needed, I suggest, is the abandonment of this whole way of looking at prayer and the substitution of ideas which are untainted by the Magnus image.

It is not the purpose of this chapter to *commend* the practice of any particular form of prayer; my task is to elucidate what prayer needs to be if it is to count as 'religious'. Let us accept, then, that it should not be viewed as a request to a supernatural being to make things different from what they would have been. Instead it needs to be associated with the way of silence. This does not preclude those who so wish from qualifying the silence by using the language of mythoi, provided only that they recognise the mythoi for what they are.

As an example it may be helpful to consider the situation where a worshipping group wishes to 'remember' or 'hold in mind' a particular individual. What is involved in that case is the carrying out of ritual in accordance with particular mythoi; and such ritual may be considered appropriate regardless of whether the person's health improves, remains the same, or deteriorates.

I should like at this point to introduce the term 'performatory language'. It is a term owes its origin to J.L. Austin (note 8.6). Austin points out that when we produce utterances such as 'I agree' or 'I promise' the function of these words is not to convey information about our state of mind: it is rather that we are in effect *expressing* agreement or *making* the promise. It is something which could also have been done by signing a document, raising our hand, or simply nodding. Implicit in the notion of performatory language there is often the presence of the word 'hereby'. Thus when we say 'I promise' this means in effect 'I hereby promise, while if we say 'I declare the meeting closed' this means 'I hereby declare the meeting closed'.

When religious ritual involves the use of words it is helpful to think of these words as constituting performatory language. Thus if we say 'We praise thee, O God' (note 8.7) we are thereby performing the act of praising, while if we say 'God be merciful to me, a sinner' (note 8.8) we are thereby carrying out a ritual in which we ask for God's mercy.

If we take seriously the way of silence it also follows that all prayers need to be agnostic as regards their effects. If this were not so they would cease to be religious in character but would simply be a means (whether effective or not) of getting something done. The performance of a ritual is no more and no less valuable whatever its outcome in terms of the person's health (note 8.9).

Many years ago I read an anthology of aphorisms which contained the words, 'God always answers prayer but sometimes the answer is "no"'. If this aphorism is expressive of a religious commitment there can be no possible objection to it. There is objection only if the words are offered as a statement of fact, or hypothesis, about a particular person or 'being' ('Magnus', if you like). In that case they are potentially misleading, since they are

55

functioning as a defence of the claim 'God always answers prayer' in a context where no counter-evidence is possible. In the absence of such possibility the alleged hypothesis fraudulent (note 8.10).

To sum up: if prayer language is to count as 'religious' it will need to have the following characteristics: (1) whatever the words used there will be an implicit recognition of the need for silence; (2) it will be couched in the language of profound truth, not the language of standard truth, and (3) it may well make use of a coherent body of mythoi such as those of the Christian tradition.

CHAPTER 9

Miracles in Magnus terms

ONE PART OF the alleged dispute between 'theism' and 'atheism' centres round the issue of miracles. There are, it seems, two conflicting views, one side contending that miracles are possible, the other side contending that they are not. I shall argue in this chapter that if the issues are posed in this way the result is deadlock. Once again it is the malign influence of Magnus which is at work.

Magnus has been defined as a non-material, supernatural being. If we think in 'Magnus' terms, therefore, we must think of a miracle as an interference with nature by supernatural power (note 9.1). Just as the force of, say, a metal spring can bring about movements of 'matter', so in the same way, it is supposed, 'non-physical' or 'non-material' forces can be brought to bear on the 'physical' world. Non-physical forces, it seems, initiated by Magnus, cause breaks in the otherwise orderly processes of nature.

The argument on the one side is that only those with closed minds or blinkered vision suppose that such forces cannot exist; on the other side it is that there is no evidence for such forces other than the credulous assertions of people who lived in a prescientific age. If the dispute is conducted in these terms it is hard to see how one side could ever convince the other. There is, once again, the 'deadlock' situation.

To bring out the absurdity of the terms of this debate my suggestion is that both parties should think through in detail what their claims involve. Suppose it is claimed that a particular event – say, the escape of the British troops from Dunkirk in 1940 (note 9.2) – occurred because God decreed a change in the weather. In that case we need to ask, What exactly happened? *Ex hypothesi* we are talking here not about the normal run of the weather – about what would have occurred in the absence of such activity by God – but about the activity itself and the events immediately before and after it.

If God caused the weather to be different from what it otherwise would have been, this presupposes that at some point there was a break in the causal chain of events (note 9.3). In that case we need to ask, If someone had been present at the appropriate location, what would they have observed? Since the issue has been assumed to be one of fact, there must necessarily have been a location of some kind as well as a particular moment in time recordable by a timing device.

Perhaps when we think along these lines there is at the back of our minds something analogous to the activity of humans; for example someone might consciously interfere in order to stop a ball from rolling down a slope. Might it not be, then, that God performs similar conscious 'acts'? If a human being interferes with the movement of a ball, those influenced by post-16th century ways of thinking may be tempted to say that this is a case of the interaction of mind and matter – a 'mental' occurrence in the form of an act of will which influences 'physical' happenings. Similarly if someone chooses to raise their finger and successfully does so it would again be thought of as a case of mind interacting with matter. May it not therefore be that the great divine 'mind' sometimes pokes 'non-physical' fingers into the 'physical' world?

Even, however, if this kind of contrast between 'the physical' and 'the non-physical' has some justification, which seems highly questionable (note 9.4), it is still misleading to describe the situation in this way. If humans intervene with events in nature we know what such intervention is like. We can observe a particular individual at work and we can observe the bodily movements which he performs in order to bring about particular effects. Magnus, however, as I have defined him, is a being who is invisible and non-material, and no such 'pay-off' observation is therefore possible. We are again confronted with the image of the hidden puppeteer, with all its attendant difficulties as described in chapters 4 and 6. If something happened which seemed to constitute a 'break' in the normal continuity of nature there would still be nothing in the situation which would entitle us to say, 'This is due to the intervention of God'.

The same difficulty applies in the case of the so-called 'miracles' reported in the gospels. As has been pointed out already (chapter 2), the events described were not at the time thought of as 'supernatural', since the contrast between 'natural' and 'supernatural' had not arisen. They were unusual events, certainly; but what the gospel writers were primarily interested in was that they were 'signs' ('semeia') which testified to the greatness of Jesus (note 9.5).

As with the idea of divine intervention at Dunkirk (see above), those who claim that the so-called miracles as reported in the gospels are records of fact are logically committed to specifying what exactly happened. As an example I should like to illustrate this point with reference to the alleged 'miracle' of the virgin birth.

If the traditional story is correct then what would have been observed at a particular point in time was a newborn child lying in a manger. However, one needs also to ask what were the events which took place somewhat earlier. Presumably the birth was like any other birth, with the usual period of gestation. But what gave rise to the period of gestation? If one wishes to claim that the virgin birth was a historical fact this question is inevitable. Somewhere along the line, it seems, the ordinary processes of conception and birth must have been interrupted. The end product may have been that Jesus' biochemistry was no different from anyone else's; but if his birth did not occur through the normal processes, then some suitably programmed sperm *must have appeared from nowhere.*

It is here that there is perhaps scope for the loaded expression 'conjuring trick'. David Jenkins, the former Bishop of Durham, is said to have used this expression in connection with the resurrection. His argument, if I have understood it, was this: if the all-important point about the resurrection is its literal truth, this is tantamount to saying that it was no more than a conjuring trick with bones; and since to say this is clearly absurd and disparaging, the original premise, viz. that the literal truth of the story is all-important, must itself be called in question. David Jenkins, it seems to me, was making a plea – wholly in line with what any Anglican bishop might have said – that it is the *religious* significance of the resurrection narrative, rather than its historicity, which needs to be emphasised (note 9.6). By the same logic, if one believes in the literal truth of the virgin birth it is hard to see how the event can be regarded as anything other than a conjuring trick with sperm.

Once again, therefore, there is evidence of the way in which we can mislead ourselves if we think in 'Magnus' terms. In the case of the virgin birth Magnus intervened to produce some sperm from nowhere; in the case of the resurrection he intervened so as to cause some bones to disappear. In both cases the events were supernatural and non-material. My plea is that we should lay these absurd images aside. Instead we need to start thinking about what the accounts of the virgin birth and resurrection have to tell us.

In the era during which the books of the bible were being written few thinkers drew a distinction between language which was designed to record historical facts and language designed to proclaim a message. Now that we are in a position to do so, however, there must surely be a strong case for saying that what is important is not the facts as such but their religious message.

This is particularly apparent in the case of St. John's gospel. Its insights relate, not to certain historical persons in the first century AD but to all of us. This can easily be shown by a number of examples, for instance: 'He must increase, but I must decrease' (note 9.7); 'Whereas I was blind, now I see (note 9.8); 'Sayest thou this thing of thyself, or did others tell it thee of me? (note 9.9). These passages commend to us the abandonment of self, the need for further spiritual enlightenment, and the importance of personal religious search. Those who say that they would be uneasy if it were shown that the so-called miracles recorded in the gospels did not 'really happen' must surely agree on reflection that it is the religious message of the above passages which is important, not their historical accuracy.

If, then, we argue that the message to be learned from the story of the virgin birth is one of profound truth it is unnecessary and irrelevant to look closely into the question, 'What exactly happened?'. If the writers of the first and third gospels (the only two to mention the virgin birth) had been aware of the laws of genetics, DNA, etc., they might conceivably have chosen a different way of calling attention to the profound truths which they wished to safeguard, but it seems very doubtful if an accurate account of the physiology of reproduction would have been all that relevant to their purposes (note 9.10).

At this point I should like to quote a set of religious relections by a contemporary writer in which he shows how Origen and Augustine emphasise the need to go beyond the literal gospel narrative and search for a deeper meaning (note 9.11):

> In 230 AD, in his *First Principles*, Origen wrote: '...*(the holy spirit's) aim is to envelop and hide secret mysteries in ordinary words under the pretext of a narrative of some kind and of an account of visible things...*' Later, in AD 416, Augustine... was likewise preaching to his congregation at Hippo about the need to seek the deeper meaning behind the Bible stories about miracles. Here he is explaining to them that the turning of the water into wine at Cana (John, 2) means the turning of the water of the Old Testament into the wine of the New by reinterpretation of the scriptures...' *Who does not wonder at water being turned into wine although God is doing this every year in the vines? Now let us begin to uncover the hidden meaning of the mysteries (for belief without understanding is milk for infants, not solid food for grown men) when the veil (over the Old Testament) is taken away so likewise is tastelessness taken away. And that which was water now becomes wine to thee. Read all the·prophetic books, and if Christ be not understood therein, what cans't thou find so insipid and silly'.*

If St. Augustine were preaching to-day no doubt the media would inform us, 'Bishop says Bible insipid and silly'.

However, it is not only in St.John's gospel that the 'message' (or, as I would call it, the profound truth) seems to take precedence over the history. It is clear on examination that the function of the other three gospels was not simply to report facts but to convey a message – that Jesus, though he met his death by crucifixion, was the promised messiah – the son of God (compare Mark 1.1 in which the proclamation is clearly set out). The 'signs and wonders' and the 'mighty works' to which the gospel writers refer were seen as a testimony to Jesus' greatness and were therefore an integral part of the gospel message. To suppose, however, that the people of this age were familiar in any explicit way with the idea of 'scientific laws' is to read into the situation ideas that did not arise until after the 16th century A.D. Still less can one suppose that they thought in terms of a supernatural being who from time to time suspended these laws.

There is no need, as far as this chapter is concerned, to attempt to take sides on issues of history – that is, on whether some or all of the events described in the gospels 'really happened'. It is not part of my task to try to influence the reader on the question of how the evidence should be interpreted. Issues of this kind belong in the area of standard truth, and no one should feel guilty for doing the best they can with the evidence available. The question of whether it can ever make sense for a religious organisation to *require* its members to believe in any particular issues of fact will be discussed in chapter 12.

Nor is it my purpose to commend any particular form of profound language, eg. that which acknowledges the 'saving grace' of Jesus. These are issues which readers must decide for themselves. My purpose has been to make a different point, viz. that, whatever the events which took place, it is unhelpful – indeed unedifying – to describe them in 'Magnus' terms – that is, in terms of a supernatural agency interfering with the course of nature. I am in effect making a plea to my readers that they should recognise religious language for what it is rather than try to defend it or find fault with it for what it is not.

CHAPTER 10

Other issues in Magnus terms

THIS CHAPTER IS concerned with some further issues connected
with Christian doctrines. My thesis is that if these doctrines
are interpreted in 'Magnus' terms, they are absurd. If, however,
they are interpreted as profound language then it is entirely open
to thoughtful people to accept them.

The doctrines which I shall discuss are those of creation, revelation, incarnation, eternal life, hell, atonement, and grace.

Creation

In the beginning God created the heaven and the earth.
And the earth was without form, and void; and dark-
ness was upon the face of the deep. And the Spirit of
God moved upon the face of the waters. And God said,
Let there be light: and there was light (note 10.1)

If we discuss creation in 'Magnus' terms then what is needed is
to discover what exactly happened. The language game might in
that case take the following form or a similar one: there was – or
possibly was not – a 'big bang' or some comparable occurrence as
a result of which the universe came into existence; and it may – or
may not – be true that the 'big bang' was planned by an intelligent
being, viz. Magnus.

However, if the issues are presented in this way the objections
to the Magnus image which have already been set out are again
applicable. Given that there are apparent signs of purpose or intelligent planning, one might be tempted to discuss whether an explanation in terms of divine purpose is or is not more convincing than

an explanation in terms of natural selection. However there is still no specification of the 'pay-off' observations that would show a divine being actually at work; and in the absence of such specification we are back with the image of the hidden puppeteer (see chapter 6). In any case a being who was responsible for setting off a 'big bang' or the like would not necessarily be an object of worship: his actions (or hers or its?) would simply be one event among others in a long chain, being unique only in that it marked some kind of 'start' (note 10.2).

The importance of the distinction between scientific (or 'empirical') issues has been brought out in a very interesting way in a broadcast discussion on creation which took place in the 1950s between Professor Flew (A.F) and Professor Mackinnon (D.M) (note 10.3). Challenged as to whether he believed in the literal historical truth of the opening chapters of *Genesis*, Professor Mackinnon replied:

> D.M. No, I wouldn't want for one moment to treat the narrative as literal: it's not that sort of thing at all... The absolute lordship of (the Jewish) God Jahweh over the world and, I would say, his authorship of *all* that was: these were the axioms of their thought and judgment. And it is in the light of this that we should interpret the language of *Genesis*....

Somewhat later the dialogue continues as follows:

> A. F. A story may be a myth: but not every myth is a *mere* myth... Perhaps it would help to define two senses of the word 'creation'. In the first, the popular sense questions about whether the world was or was not created are questions to which the latest news from the science front is relevant...In the second, the theological sense, questions about creation are questions about an absolute ontological dependence to which particular scientific discoveries are simply irrelevant. This distinction is important: but difficult, because almost everyone – including St. Thomas – who has believed in creation in the second sense has also believed that the world had a beginning, and that it was in the first sense, also, created.

D.M. Yes, I think that one is always conscious in reading Aquinas here that he lived in an age before the distinction between the domain of the scientist and that
of the metaphysician had been drawn. We live in a more
sophisticated age. However, I think that a Thomist
would say that there was a kind of fundamental understanding of one's creaturely lot that was independent
of the movement of empirical discovery... It is a matter
of having a sense of being a created being. What I want
to do is to get to grips with the meaning of this kind of
language. Language whereby we, so to speak, take up
the posture proper to us, indicate the sort of beings we
are. *Either* we must use in these contexts words borrowed from the familiar transactions of experience, *or*
we must say nothing at all.

Mackinnon is here emphasising the non-literal nature of religious
discourse ('words borrowed from the familiar transactions of
experience') – a point which, as was noted in chapter 5, many
contemporary thinkers appear to have overlooked.

To sum up: if we interpret the doctrine of creation in 'Magnus'
terms, that is, as standard truth, this logically commits us to adjust-
ing our beliefs in the light of the most recent scientific discoveries.
Moreover, in the light of the definition of 'religion' offered in this
book, no such evaluation of the evidence can be relevant to decisions about religious commitment. If, however, we interpret the
doctrine of creation as commending the mythos that we are created beings or 'creatures', standing in relation to a creator, this
mythos clearly represents a challenge to our whole way of life.

I should like to end this section on creation by quoting some
wise words of Bishop Berkeley. Obviously Berkeley's world picture
was in some respects different from our own at the present day;
and in particular one must suppose that he did not question the
account of creation as given in the first chapter of *Genesis*. He did,
however, recognise the difficulty in the supposition that at the
moment of creation things suddenly appeared from nowhere; and,
most strikingly, what was important for him was (in my terminology) the profound truth to which the doctrine of the creation gave
rise. The passage runs as follows:

In case we conceive the creation, as we should at this time a parcel of plants or vegetables of all sorts, produced by an invisible power, in a desert where no body was present: that this way of explaining or conceiving it....exactly suits with the common, natural, undebauched notions of mankind: that it manifests the dependence of all things on God; and consequently hath all the good effect or influence, which it is possible that important article of our faith should have in making men humble, thankful, and resigned to their creator (note 10.4).

Revelation

As a postscript to the discussion of creation I should like to refer briefly to the concept of *revelation*. The following is the account of 'revelation' given in the *Oxford Dictionary of the Christian Church* (note 10.5)

Since it is commonly held that there are certain truths about God which are to be learned through man's natural endowments... while others, eg the doctrine of the holy trinity, are not conceivable except by faith, Christian philosophers have often held that a sharp distinction must be made between 'truths of reason' and 'truths of revelation'.

If we think in 'Magnus' terms we will be tempted to suppose that where there has been revealed truth a Magnus-like being chose to interfere with the course of nature and by supernatural power then disclosed to us truths of which we would otherwise not have been aware.

The doctrine of creation is commonly assumed to be a truth of revelation. Thus, in a book by A.E. Taylor, an eminent Aristotle scholar (note 10.6), we are told:

The 'cosmos', or orderly world of natural processes, is strictly 'eternal'; 'motion' is everlasting and continuous, or unbroken. Even the great Christian theologians who built upon Aristotle could not absolutely break with him on this point. St. Thomas, though obliged to

66

admit that the world was actually created a few thousand years before his own time, maintains that this can only be known to be true from revelation; philosophically it is equally tenable that the world should have been 'created from all eternity'. And it is the general doctrine of scholasticism that the expression 'creation' only denotes the absolute dependence of the world on God for its being.

The last section of this passage indicates that what I would call 'Magnus' ways of thinking form no part of scholastic thought. To those, however, who nowadays think in 'Magnus' terms the objections formulated in chapters 5 and 6 of this book still apply. No 'pay-off' observation has been specified by which one could establish definitively that a non-material act of revelation had taken place; and even if this difficulty could be overcome there is no reason why the resultant message should command allegiance of a religious kind. Our knowledge of standard truth might have been increased but there would not necessarily have been any additional insight into profound truth.

Incarnation

According to the *Oxford Dictionary of the Christian Church* (note 10.7)

> the Christian doctrine of the Incarnation affirms that the eternal Son of God took human flesh from His human mother and that the historical Christ is at once fully God and fully man.

It is a doctrine which lends itself all too easily to interpretation in 'Magnus' terms. To put the matter in the crudest possible way, it would seem that Magnus took a space trip and came to live on the planet earth.

In this connection I cannot do better than quote the passage from John Robinson's *Honest to God* (note 10.8) where he makes precisely this point:

> The traditional supernaturalistic way of describing the Incarnation almost inevitably suggests that Jesus was

really God almighty walking about on earth, dressed up as a man ... He looked like a man, he talked like a man ... but underneath he was God dressed up ... However guardedly it may be stated, the traditional view leaves the impression that God took a space-trip and arrived on this planet in the form of a man. Jesus was not really one of us; but through the miracle of the Virgin Birth he contrived to be born so as to appear one of us. Really he came from outside. I am aware that this is a parody, and probably an offensive one, but I think it is perilously near the truth of what most people – and I would include myself – have been brought up to believe at Christmas time.

To an unsophisticated person in the Greek or Roman worlds in the centuries before the Christian era there would, I am sure, have been nothing particularly unusual about the idea of a god taking human form. The people of Athens believed that this was what had happened in the case of Barnabas and Paul:

They lifted up their voices, saying in the speech of Lycaonia, The gods are come down to us in the likeness of men. And they called Barnabas, Jupiter; and Paul, Mercurius, because he was the chief speaker (note 10.9)

There is in fact a well known hymn, based on the work of a writer in the fourth century A.D., which encourages this kind of view of the incarnation:

Fairer than the sun at morning
Was the star that told his birth,
To the world its God announcing
Seen in fleshly form on earth (note 10.10)

It is plain, however, that if such language is interpreted literally there is again a 'Magnus' problem – one that is basically the same as that already referred to in chapter 9. If a god took on human form there must have been some kind of continuity between the divine state and the human state and some point at which the individual stopped being a god and became a human. If, however, we try to think this idea through we must surely regard it as unintelligible.

One of the great expressions of the doctrine of the incarnation is, of course, the formula that the *word* (logos) became *flesh* (note 10.11). It is important in this connection to note that the word 'logos' in Greek does not stand for anything 'supernatural' or 'non-material' (compare chapter 2). It is a word which has a number of different senses; these include in particular that of giving a rational account of something by the use of words. We should also note that the Greek term which is usually translated as 'matter' ('hule') does not carry the 'dualistic' associations ('matter'as opposed to 'mind') which nowadays we might be tempted to bring to it. 'Hule' can in fact be thought of as the 'stuff' of which things are made – the 'raw material', if you like. The contrasting term is 'eidos' (approximately 'form' or 'shape'): it is its eidos which makes something this kind of object rather than that. Although the words 'became flesh' may in our era have overtones which suggest that the non-material turned into something material, it seems clear that this way of thinking would have made no sense in the first century A.D. Moreover even in our own day it is pertinent to ask if this idea is intelligible, since the question inevitably arises, What exactly happened at the moment of transition? When one is logically forced to ask an absurd question it is right to suspect that there is something wrong with one's premises.

If, however, the doctrine of creation is interpreted as mythos the problem of 'continuity' (how a god or the logos turned into a human being) does not arise, since as far as the insights provided by the mythos is concerned the matter is irrelevant. Whatever one's view as to the facts about the historical Jesus – which depends on one's evaluation of the evidence – there is nothing logically inappropriate in making a religious commitment in which the mythoi of incarnation, grace, forgiveness, and the like play a major part. It is only if we think in 'Magnus' terms that we will be tempted to suppose that at a particular time in history a supernatural being came to live among humans.

Eternal life

In the *Oxford Dictionary of the Christian Church* (note 10.12) 'eternal life' is described as

69

... the fullness of life of which the believer becomes possessed here and now through participation in God's eternal being

If we think in 'Magnus' terms, however, the picture is very different. We must suppose, it seems, that an 'immaterial' part of our personality, the soul, survives death. As we saw in chapter 2, this way of thinking was not unknown in Greek times, and in fact it has been influential in western thought in many different ways. Here, as an example, are some of the reflections of Marlowe's Faustus before the devils carry him off:

> Ah, Pythagoras' metempsychosis, were that true,
> This soul should fly from me, and I be chang'd
> Unto some brutish beast! All beasts are happy,
> For, when they die,
> Their souls are soon dissolv'd in elements;
> But mine must live, still to be plagu'd in hell (note 10.13)

Even in present-day hymns references to 'soul and body' are not uncommon, as in:

> On the resurrection morning
> Soul and body meet again.
> No more sorrow, no more weeping
> No more pain (note 10.14)

There are, however, the usual 'Magnus'-type objections to such a view. First, one can ask, What would it be *like* for a soul to leave a body – what would be the 'pay-off' observation which justified the use the words, 'A soul is now leaving a body' (note 10.15); and if no answer is given we are again misleading ourselves with words. Secondly, it is hard to envisage such a happening as anything but a clever conjuring trick; and in that case it would at best be an example of a standard truth and would not necessarily give us any insight into profound truth.

Belief in the immortality of the soul, however, has in fact never formed part of orthodox Christianity; the Apostles' creed, for example, speaks not of the immortality of the soul but of the resurrection of the body. The words of Professor J.V. Langmead Casserley (note 10.16) seem to me particularly relevant here. Casserley disputes the value of asking whether

70

a part of man, called his 'mind', has within it some inherent property which gives it the power to survive the dissolution of the body.... The problem for the Christian is whether God can and will revive mortal man, and lift him above time and make him a partaker of eternal life.

This is the language of profound truth, not of unsubstantiated guesses about what will happen after death.

The same is true of the well known passages in St.John's gospel:

I give unto them eternal life; and they shall never perish, neither shall any man pluck them out of my hand (note 10.17)

and

I am the resurrection, and the life: he that believeth in me, though he were dead, yet shall he live: And whoso-ever liveth and believeth in me shall never die. Believest thou this? (note 10.18).

To live by these profound truths does not commit anyone to a belief that Magnus carries out some non-physical actions by which people's souls survive the dissolution of their bodies.

Confronted with the mysteries of life and death there is, strictly speaking, no option for any of us but silence. If, however, we break the silence by bringing in the mythos of resurrection, with all that this implies, then our silence can properly be called 'religious'.

Hell

If the doctrine of hell is understood in 'Magnus' terms there are again the familiar difficulties. In the words of Professor Ian Ramsey:

If there is a Hell in the sense of some place in a life after death for endless punishment, where do we locate such a hell? Further, so far as time goes, have we to suppose that its time series is continuous with the time which we know in human life? In other words, to be at all clear and effective as a doctrine, Hell presupposes a life *after* death largely continuous in time with life *before* death, and having very similar features. Yet neither of these

71

presuppositions seems at all antecedently plausible (note 10.19)

There is also a moral objection to thinking of hell in 'Magnus' terms. If Magnus inflicts eternal torment on people this seems to imply some kind of vindictiveness on Magnus' part. Even if punishment for a limited time sometimes has moral justification (which is itself a contentious issue) it is hard to see how *eternal* punishment could ever be justified.

None of this means, however, that the doctrine of hell is implausible or immoral if properly stated. I return to the words of Professor Ramsey:

> One way of expressing the problem of hell is to say that it is the problem of using .... models to point to God, to talk of God, without running into discourse which is morally repugnant or blatantly inconsistent with other regions of religious discourse... So my conclusion is that all pictures which cluster around the doctrine of Hell have their point when and only when they recapture for us a disclosure of God's redeeming love.... Doctrines of Hell... also provide... a good example of how theology can be bedevilled by misunderstandings of its point, its status and its character (note 10.20).

Thinking of hell in 'Magnus' terms seems to me a good example of just such a misunderstanding. Belief in the doctrine of hell need not imply that a Magnus-like being commits people to eternal torment, still less that he derives any enjoyment from doing so (note 10.21). The profound truth which the doctrine attempts to express is the mythos that God is holy – from which it follows that pride, selfishness, cruelty and the like cannot simply be brushed aside as unimportant. This type of language can properly be described as 'religious'.

Atonement

The Oxford Dictionary of the Christian Church (note 10.22) speaks of

> ... (i.e. 'at-one-ment')... man's reconciliation with God through the sacrificial death of Christ.

If, however, we think of the atonement in 'Magnus' terms this commits us to supposing that expressions such as 'the washing away of sins' have to be taken literally. Again the objections are twofold.

First, on a literal interpretation one would have to suppose a kind of purifying on the part of Magnus. On this view, having come to live among humans he did something which brought about our forgiveness. 'Natural' means could not have achieved this: the power which he exerted had therefore to be supernatural and non-material. *What* was done, and how it achieved the effect which it did would still be puzzling.

If we reflect, however, I think it will become clear that the analogy of a cure brought about by unknown means is not a valid one. If we do not know how something was done this standardly means that its way of working could in principle be discovered. In this case, however, no specification is given even of what would *count* as an appropriate way of working; by implication one is postulating activity of the part of a hidden puppeteer.

In addition there are the same moral difficulties. In thinking about the atonement it is very easy to be influenced by the image of the 'whipping boy' (note 10.23). Let me explain. The story goes that the boy king, Edward VI, sometimes misbehaved; and it was taken for granted that misbehaviour on anyone's part merits punishment. However, it was thought grossly improper to whip his majesty; and for this reason a substitute victim had to be found – a boy who was employed to 'bear the punishment' which by rights should have been inflicted on the young king!

I know of those who have objected to the doctrine of the atonement because they interpreted it in 'whipping boy' terms; and if this were what the doctrine of the atonement involved it would, indeed, be scandalously immoral.

This, however, is to suppose that a Magnus-like being has been at work. What is needed – as in the case of the other doctrines considered in this chapter – is to ask what are the profound truths to which the doctrine of the atonement points.

To answer this question it is necessary to consider the biblical context which alone can make sense of the doctrine. Central to this context is the view that

73

all have sinned and fallen short of the glory of God

(note 10.24)

and that

the wages of sin is death (note 10.25)

What we have earned, therefore, according to this mythos, is death – to be interpreted, perhaps, as separation from God. However a free gift is on offer to all of us if we choose to take it up. If we do so we are saved not because of our deserts but because of the infinite love of God. To choose to live by this mythos is neither 'unscientific' (since the issue is not one of science) nor logically absurd.

Grace

It is standard Christian doctrine that because of the sin of Adam man is a 'fallen' being; only, therefore, by grace can he be restored to a right relationship with God.

If, however, we think in 'Magnus' terms it is all too easy to suppose that 'grace' is the name of some non-material 'stuff' which is made available to people on special occasions. Thus if someone is confronted with a particularly demanding task one might be tempted to express hope not only that that person will show perseverance, wisdom, and the like but that their efforts will be supported by the supernatural effects of God's 'grace'. Similarly, if a child is being baptised, there would be the hope that 'supernatural' forces will operate in protecting her from evil.

To this way of viewing the matter there are the usual objections. One cannot say whether or not such non-material 'stuff' is exerting some influence unless criteria are specified, in terms of a pay-off observation, for recognising its influence. There is also the by now familiar moral objection: that this special help should be dispensed only on particular occasions seems unfair – and, indeed, might be thought to give the recipient an unfair advantage compared with his fellow human beings! Also it seems immoral that people should be judged favourably not because of anything that they have done but because an external agency – the holy spirit – has been good to them (note 10.26).

74

The profound truth underlying the doctrine of grace is of course quite different. To understand it we need to immerse ourselves in the 'language games' in which it is used. Here are some relevant passages from a variety of religious writings:

> By grace are ye saved through faith; and that, not of yourselves: it is the gift of God (note 10.27)

> The scanty triumphs grace hath won
> The broken vow, the frequent fall (note 10.28)

These two passages underline that grace is not something which we have earned. In the words of a well known hymn:

> Could my tears for ever flow,
> Could my zeal no respite know,
> All for sin could not atone;
> Thou must save and thou alone (note 10.29)

A helpful analogy in terms of human relationships is the situation where one is willing not just to admit one's errors but to stop trying to justify oneself. 'Use every man after his desert', says Hamlet, 'and who should 'scape whipping?' (note 10.30). If we think of the analogy of a courtroom the situation would be one in which we do not attempt self-defence but throw ourselves on the mercy of the judge.

In brief, interpreted in 'Magnus' terms the doctrine of grace is both logically self-defeating and immoral. If it is interpreted as the language of profound truth, however, the same objections no longer apply.

———————

It has not been the purpose of this chapter to commend the profound truths of which it gives examples; my purpose has been to elucidate these truths and show that they need not be tied to 'Magnus' ways of thinking. If they were, they would be both immoral and incredible.

CHAPTER 11

God and evil

IF WE NO LONGER THINK of God as a 'Magnus'-like figure it becomes possible to view the so-called 'problem of evil' in something of a new light.

A formulation of the problem in traditional terms might run something like this. It is claimed that God is all-good, all-powerful, and all-knowing. Yet if he had been all-good he would not have allowed any evil to occur; if he had been all-powerful he would have been able to prevent it, and if he had been all-knowing he would have foreseen it in the first place; there is therefore a contradiction in professing to believe in a God who combines these three attributes. The challenge, therefore, to self-professed theists is to explain how they can hold these three beliefs simultaneously when, as a matter of logic, at least one of them must be false.

Various answers have been suggested. One could, of course, break the deadlock by saying either that God is not all-good or that he is not all-powerful. However this solution appears to be at variance with traditional Christian teaching. A commonly preferred solution is to say that one way in which God has shown his goodness is to give people free will: if they then choose evil this is not something for which God can be blamed. According to this argument, it is a matter of logic, not a limitation of God's power, to say that he 'cannot' both allow free will and prevent the consequences of that freedom. Nonsense remains nonsense even if it is prefixed with the words 'God can....' (note 11.1). This argument is not without interest, but even if it is a way of explaining the evils that result from human agency there are still many evils – plagues, earthquakes, etc. – for which human weakness cannot be blamed.

76

The trouble is that the traditional 'Magnus' view creates its own problems – which then require dubious logical manoeuvres in order to escape from them! These manoeuvres inevitably seem like sophistry, and it is not clear that they have anything to do with religion. If, however, we reject the Magnus image it follows that the notions of 'all-goodness', 'omnipotence', and 'omniscience' can no longer be taken literally. Instead what we are left with is a group of mythoi about God which may contain references to the everyday concepts of 'goodness', 'power', and 'knowledge'; and it is then possible by a leap of the imagination to think of the power and knowledge as 'unlimited'. This is an insight which we in fact owe to Bishop Berkeley, who wrote:

> Taking the word *idea* in a large sense, my soul may be said to furnish me with an idea, that is, an image, or likeness of God, though indeed extremely inadequate; for all the notion I have of God, is obtained by reflecting on my own soul, heightening its powers, and removing its imperfections (note 11.2)

Berkeley's statement represents a clear recognition of the fact that the words 'all-good', 'all-powerful', and 'all-knowing' cannot be taken at their face value. We know, as human beings, what a series is, and we can conceive of a series being carried on indefinitely; what we cannot conceive of is such a series coming to an end.

One of the difficulties about many discussions of 'the problem of evil' is that they have become highly intellectualised and, as a consequence, seem to have little to do with the religious life. I have in mind questions such as, 'Since God is omnipotent he must have foreseen the sin of Adam – and in that case why didn't he do anything about it?' If we turn to the actual evil in the world we are confronted with something very different.

In the case, for instance, of the holocaust, or indeed of any situation in which innocent people are taken to their deaths, we need to ask, What kind of response could properly be termed 'religious'? Those who think in 'Magnus' terms, if their task is to comfort the bereaved, are logically committed to telling the person what the 'facts' are about death and a future life with as much conviction as they can muster – and many people, I am sure, would, acknowledge the inappropriateness of so doing. If, however, we reject 'Magnus' ways of thinking the position is different. None of us is in any position to claim that we have any additional facts at our disposal of a comforting kind: a response which could properly be termed 'religious' might consist of silence, or perhaps of a handshake or some other indication of sympathy. In other contexts it might comprise the recall of those mythoi which to a given individual were most meaningful. To a Christian believer, for instance, one might offer the words:

'Christ being raised from the dead dieth no more; death hath no more dominion over him' (note 11.3)

In a different context it might be helpful to consider 'the problem of evil' as it presented itself to some of the old testament writers. A question which continually arose was – Why should Jehovah allow his chosen people to suffer?

Thou art of purer eyes than to behold evil, and canst not look on iniquity: wherefore lookest thou upon them that deal treacherously, and holdest thy tongue when the wicked devoureth the man that is more righteous than he? (note 11.4).

It was possible to believe that all would come right in the long run. One might see

'the ungodly in great power: and flourishing like a green bay-tree' (note 11.5);

but it was still possible to say – perhaps with misguided optimism -

I have been young, and now am old: yet saw I never the righteous forsaken, nor his seed begging their bread (note 11.6).

As has been noted already (chapter 5) the book of Job raises the problem of evil in all its starkness.

Confronted with other kinds of evil – for example a human being reduced to a 'vegetable' state as a result of birth injury or later accident – a religious way of responding might be to express awe or even indignation – 'Why has God permitted this?' (note 11.7). The very fact that it is possible to express such indignation is for some people the expression of an important religious truth.

To sum up: if we think about 'the problem of evil' in 'Magnus' terms we are logically obliged to take the notions of 'all-goodness', 'omnipotence' and 'omniscience' literally, and in that case we are confronted with insoluble intellectual difficulties as to how an all-good, omnipotent and omniscient being can permit evil. The damage, however, is self-inflicted: if God is thought of in 'Magnus' terms there is no way round the contradiction. In contrast, a religious response is one which may fumblingly tell mythoi about the evils in the world but does not make any factual claims about a 'being' who – in a literal sense of the words – 'caused' or 'permitted' these evils.

CHAPTER 12

Beyond theism and atheism

IF THE ARGUMENTS in this book are correct then disputes between theists and atheists, as currently conducted, can be put behind us once for all.

The words 'as currently conducted' are important. There are, indeed, differences between theists and atheists; but it is not that one side or the other has 'got their facts wrong' as to whether a supernatural being does or does not exist. As I shall argue in a moment, they are differences in the mythoi to which people choose to commit themselves.

It is, of course, clear that many thoughtful Christians are well aware of the problems which arise if we talk about God's 'existence' in a literal sense. My purpose in the book has not been to find fault with such people but to encourage them to go further down the same road – to leave literalness even further behind them. Just as 'father', 'right hand', etc. are inadequate ways of speaking about God, so also are the words 'exist', real' and 'fact'.

One of the issues here is a trivial matter of linguistic decision. If discussions of theism and atheism are assumed to be inextricably tied to 'Magnus' ways of thinking, then one can quite properly speak of the need to go *beyond* theism and atheism since both views alike are mistaken. An alternative, however, is to describe as theists those who accept and live by particular mythoi – for instance the mythos of the loving father who 'took our nature upon him' and gave his life for our redemption. By contrast, in that case, an atheist would be one who did not take such mythoi seriously. If this way of speaking is adopted there is, indeed, a difference between theism and atheism, but the difference lies in people's choice of mythoi: it is not that theists believe in a supernatural being and atheists do not.

There is also need for a similar verbal decision over the word 'prayer'. I have met people who say, 'I don't believe in the sort of God that you pray to'; and for such people the notion of prayer is so tied to 'Magnus' ways of thinking that they prefer to say that they 'don't pray'. An alternative is to reinterpret the word 'prayer' along the lines indicated in chapter 8, in which case those who pray are not addressing someone who 'exists' in a literal sense: rather, they are carrying out rituals involving particular mythoi, for instance expressing gratitude for their 'creation, preservation, and all the blessings of this life' (note 12.1), holding in mind relatives or friends whom they love, dedicating themselves anew to the tasks ahead of them, or perhaps simply asking their heavenly father to give them their daily bread. Such rituals would, of course, cease to be religious if their aim was to change in any way the course of nature or to help people to improve their lives by means of auto-suggestion.

Once it is recognised that the language of religion is the language of profound truth rather than of standard truth, it is possible to look in a new way at the relationship between religion and science. Stark conflict between the two is ruled out, since as a matter of logic no profound truth can be disproved by a standard truth. However, it is arguable that scientific findings offer us what may be called an 'invitation' to view the world in a particular way. Thus, on the one hand, people may feel disposed to *marvel* at the wonders of science – at the intricacies of biological organisms, for instance, or at the vast distances of outer space; and if such people are disposed to say with the psalmist:

The heavens declare the glory of God (note 12.2)

they are in no way being 'unscientific' since they are not claiming anything which belongs within the scientific 'language game'. There may, however, be others who take the view that life is

... a tale
Told by an idiot, full of sound and fury,
Signifying nothing (note 12.3)

Again there is nothing in scientific discovery, as such, which either requires people to adopt this view or is incompatible with their doing so.

It may still be objected that there is a possible source of conflict between science and religion if religious organisations require their members to believe things which science shows to be mistaken. Might this not be the case, for instance (to take two examples for illustration purposes only), if a religious organisation required its members to deny the theory of evolution or to believe that the world was created in six days around 4004 B.C.?

If my argument is right, however, this conflict is a spurious one. In the first place, an organisation which requires its members to believe that certain facts are the case is not imposing a *religious* demand, since matters of fact come within the domain of standard and not profound truth. More importantly, however, there is the question of what sense can be attached to the idea of *requiring* somebody to take a particular line on some matter of fact. The issue here is not whether it is wise, proper, prudent etc. for a religious body to do so but whether as a matter of logic such an expression is coherent.

Lewis Carroll cleverly exploited this logical point in the following passage of *Through the Looking Glass*:

> Alice laughed. 'There's no use trying,' she said; 'one *can't* believe impossible things.'
> 'I daresay you haven't had much practice,' said the Queen. 'When I was your age, I always did it for half-an-hour a day. Why, sometimes I've believed as many as six impossible things before breakfast' (note 12.4).

It makes logical sense to ask people to *go through the motions* of saying that they believe certain facts to be the case (however pointless such a requirement might be), but as a point of logic 'believing' is not the sort of thing that one do or fail to do to order: the only way to make a judgment on an issue of fact is by considering the evidence, and if the evidence is compelling there is no more to be said. Even, therefore, if particular religious bodies were to *claim* that they required their members to take a particular line on some issue of fact, this cannot as a matter of logic be what they are doing: their error is one of logic, not of policy (note 12.5).

There is another consequence of my argument which needs to be touched on. It relates to the ambiguities which necessarily arise in the interpretation of answers to questionnaires or social surveys. People are sometimes asked – without qualification or explanation – *'whether they believe in God'* and questions of a like kind; and this is regularly assumed to be an indication of their religious commitment.

Now if religious commitment were the same thing as believing that a Magnus-like being existed this might, indeed, be the case. However it has been my contention throughout the book that discussion in these terms trivialises reltgion; and as an illustration of this point I cannot do better than quote the following words written by my friend, Stephen Mitchell, an Anglican clergyman:

> Like the Sirens, commonsense seduces voyagers from their journeys of exploration. Faith then becomes trapped in the alluring questions of the TV presenter and opinion pollster. Do you believe in God? Do you believe in life after death? Do you believe in the Virgin Birth? Say yes to at least eight out of ten and you'll be put down as a believer. Score less than five and you're sunk (note 12.6).

If the argument of this book is correct the language of profound truth is not something which can be 'bandied about' in this way.

The sub-title of the book refers both to theism and to atheism; and since up to now it is theism which has received the most attention; I should like now to say a few words in order to redress the balance.

My impression is that, apart from a few 'campaigners', the number of people who explicitly say that they 'do not believe in God' is relatively small. What we find is that there are plenty of people who 'vote with their feet' in the sense that they rarely attend a place of worship or do so only on special occasions such as baptisms, weddings, and funerals. Their reasons may be varied – and may include, for instance, force of habit, indifference, or the competing demands of other commitments. There is therefore a risk of misleading oneself if one talks of 'the' atheist in a stereotyped way. Nevertheless it makes sense to consider some of the things which might be said by a thoughtful individual whose views, whether explicitly or implicitly, were 'atheistic' in outlook.

Now it seems to me plain that what the great majority of self-professed atheists are objecting to is the Magnus image Such people assume that 'belief in God' entails belief in a supernatural being – and this is something that they find impossible to accept (note 12.7). For such people this book has a simple message: 'you are quite right to object to the "Magnus" image but this need not preclude you, if you are so minded, from taking part in religious worship'. One could even say that mythoi need not be explicit and that everyone, whatever they profess to believe, will be living out certain values and therefore implicitly living according to certain mythoi. The word 'atheist' could therefore be used to refer to those who, explicitly or implicitly, choose not to live by the mythos of the loving father. This would not, of course, necessarily mean that their values were all that different from those for whom this mythos was of prime importance (note 12.8).

In this connection I recently came on a letter in the press from Harry Stopes-Roe, vice president of the British Humanist Association:

> The justification for RE {religious education} is that it helps pupils to understand the ultimate questions of living: life and death, the importance of morality, the reality (or otherwise) of God (note 12.9).

If it is typical of humanists or atheists in general, this letter disposes of any suggestion that their values are radically different from those who would describe themselves as religiously committed. It seems to me that once there is agreement on the need to reject the 'Magnus' image a central source of disputation is removed.

A final question requires discussion, viz. Can the views expressed in this book rebut the charge of what may be called 'religious relativism'? Given that there is no obvious way of determining why one mythos should be preferable to another, are we not reduced to saying that the issue is nothing more than a matter of personal taste, like, for example, one person's preference for oranges and another person's preference for apples? Am I not committed to saying that the mythos of the god who gave himself for our redemption is all right for some without being mandatory for all?

What is important here is to emphasise the need for silence. Any mythos will of necessity be inadequate; but it is nevertheless possible to accept a particular group of mythoi – for instance those of the Christian tradition – as sincere attempts, however fumbling, to say something important. In this area there is no certainty, but to point this out is not the same thing as saying, 'It is all relative' or 'It is all a matter of opinion'.

In scientific enquiry open-mindedness and a willingness to consider evidence that seemingly counts against one's thesis is essential if one is not to be misled. In matters of religion, however, there is no logical absurdity or inappropriateness in being totally committed to a highly specified set of mythoi. The arguments of this book do not establish relativism; at most – since we are in an area where the notion of certainty is inappropriate – they may perhaps encourage people to take a more relaxed attitude to faiths or beliefs different from their own. There is nothing logically absurd about claiming certainty for one's religious beliefs, but from the very nature of the 'language game' which is being played there is a case for professing what has been called an 'open-minded certainty' (note 12.10) rather than an aggressive one.

Concluding remarks

Magnus has been defined as a being who is supernatural and non-material. However, since there is no word in the bible that translates as either 'supernatural' or 'non-material' (see chapter 2) readers who reject the Magnus image are not rejecting anything biblical. In addition, since most readers will be quite happy to say that God does not *literally* have a right hand, I hope it will not be too difficult a step for them to allow that expressions such as 'exists' and 'causes things to happen' should not be taken literally either. This would in fact be a recognition that it is demeaning to God to suppose that any description in human terms could be adequate.

My message for self-professed 'atheists' is that there is no need for them to think of God in 'Magnus' terms. Such people may find it helpful to reflect further on the functions and significance of religious language. Rejection of the Magnus image does not entail abandonment of religious belief in its entirety.

It has not been the purpose of this book to tell any of my readers either that their religious beliefs are adequate as they stand or that they need to be changed. My central theme has been that questions of fact have nothing to do with decisions about religious commitment. If it was *in fact* the case that a God exists there might be grounds for conditional loyalty of a kind that could quite properly be shown to any person or institution, but conditional loyalty is not the stuff of which religious commitment is made.

Finally, if anyone changes their religious practices after reading this book, so be it. I would be happier, however, if they continued with their existing practices but did so with a greater degree of understanding.

Notes

Preface note 1. J.A.T. Robinson, *Honest to God*. London:SCM Press, 1963.

Preface note 2. A. MacIntyre, 'God and the theologians'. In *The Honest to God Debate*, ed. J.A.T Robinson and D.L. Edwards. London: SCM Press, 1963, p.215.

Preface note 3. D. Cupitt, *Taking Leave of God*. London: SCM Press, 1980, p.37.

Preface note 4. *The Observer*, Sept. 4th, 1984. The headline to this piece is 'Dean called an atheist'. The author, Judith Judd, says that Cupitt's views 'make the new bishop of Durham (David Jenkins) look like a pillar of orthodoxy'.

Preface note 5. J.A.T. Robinson, Comment on 'God and the theologians'. In *The Honest to God Debate*, op.cit. pp.229-230.

Preface note 6. *Taking Leave of God*, op. cit., Preface note 3.

NOTES TO CHAPTER 1

Note 1.1. G. Ryle, *The Concept of Mind*. London: Hutchinson, 1949).

Note 1.2. It is interesting that Ryle seldom refers to his philosophical colleagues by name. There are references in *The Concept of Mind* to Aristotle, Hobbes, and Descartes; but it was very rare for him to carry out detailed analysis of arguments adduced by his contemporaries. I have not been able to follow him totally in this, but I have the same wish to avoid polemic.

Note 1.3. Edward Fitzgerald, *The Rubaiyat of Omar Khayyam*, stanza 29.

Note 1.4. Emily Brontë, *Last Lines*.

Note 1.5. *John* **viii**, 58.

Note 1.6. *John* **iv**, 14.

Note 1.7. See L. Wittgenstein, *Philosophical Investigations*, tr. G.E.M. Anscombe. Oxford: Blackwell, 1953, passim.

Note 1.8. The analogy of the 'dropping penny' was regularly used by the late bishop Ian Ramsay whose writings on the philosophy of religion were an inspiration to many people of my generation.

Note 1.9. P.G. Wodehouse, *Eggs, Beans and Crumpets* (Harmondsworth: Penguin Books, 1971), chapter 6, 'Romance at Droitgate Spa'.

Note 1.10. Compare Cupitt, *Taking Leave of God* (London: SCM Press, 1980), p.15. According to Cupitt

> Most plain men – and plain philosophers too, for that matter – take a realist view of God... Admittedly it must be allowed that God is a special case... All the same, those plain men and plain philosophers insist, whether or not there is a God remains at bottom a factual question.

Cupitt's use of the word 'realism' calls for some discussion. 'Realism' in philosophy is standardly contrasted with 'idealism' – realism being the belief that things exist independently of any observer, idealism being the belief that they are mind-dependent. It is agreed that the actual predictions made by a philosophical realist are no different from those made by a philosophical idealist; for example it is no part of the idealist's thesis that chairs are unreal in the sense that you must not talk about them or that they will vanish if you try to sit on them! By analogy, then, a theological realist is one who believe that God has an independent existence. However, in a theological context the contrasting term is not 'idealist' but 'non-realist'; and, corresponding to my rather frivolous example of vanishing chairs, a theological non-realist would be one who is quite prepared to use the word 'God' in his discourse but is not committed to the view that God is an independently existing being. For example the prayer

> God be in my head
> And in my understanding

88

need not be interpreted in realist terms since it implies nothing about an independently existing entity. In connection with his own book (ibid. p.166) Cupitt writes that he has

> conducted a long campaign against theological realism... I continue to speak of God and to pray to God. God is the mythical embodiment of all that one is concerned with in the spiritual life.

Although Cupitt has written much else since *Taking Leave of God* was published in 1984, the arguments which he puts forward in this book still constitute one of the most important statements of the case for non-realism. Chiefly so as to avoid philosophical controversy I shall not myself be using the terms 'realism' and 'non-realism' in the present book; however, if a theological non-realist is defined as one who does not treat God's existence as an issue of fact then my attack on the Magnus image can appropriately be called 'non-realist'.

Note 1.11. This characterisation of Magnus has been adopted – to use Gilbert Ryle's phrase – 'with deliberate abusiveness' (*The Concept of Mind*, p.15) – so as to enable me to poke fun at the views which I am attacking. It was with similar 'deliberate abusiveness' that Ryle coined the phrase 'the Ghost in the machine' (op.cit. pp.15-16) in order to expose a wide ranging family of philosophical errors.

Note 1.12. For further information on apophatic theology see note 7.12. Compare also note 5.18.

NOTES TO CHAPTER 2

Note 2.1. T.D. Weldon, *Introduction to Kant's Critique of Pure Reason*. Oxford: Clarendon Press, p.4. In this connection it is interesting to note that Edward Fitzgerald in his account of the life of Omar Khayyam (New York: Airmont, p.8) says that Omar, 'pretending sensual pleasure, as the serious purpose of life, only diverted himself with speculative problems of Deity, Destiny, *Matter and Spirit* {my italics}, Good and Evil, and other such questions'. That a 19th century thinker such as Fitzgerald should suppose that the issue of 'matter and spirit' was a subject of debate throughout the ages is not surprising, but it seems to me highly doubtful whether Omar, who lived in Persia in the 11th and 12th centuries, would have thought of 'matter' and 'spirit' in these terms.

Note 2.2 *Cruden's Complete Concordance to the Old and New Testaments*, by Alexander Cruden. Guildford: Lutterworth Press, 1974.

Note 2.3. *Odyssey*, Book 3, line 372.

Note 2.4. *Iliad*, Book 20, lines 66-74.

Note 2.5. *Odyssey*, Book 8, lines 266 seq.

Note 2.6. *Iliad*, Book 5, line 290.

Note 2.7. *Iliad*, Book 22, lines 361-363.

Note 2.8. *Odyssey*, Book 11, lines 204-208.

Note 2.9. Plato, *Phaedo*, section 81a.

Note 2.10. See Aristotle *De Anima*, passim. Relevant passages include Book I, 5, section 411b and Book II, 2, section 413a. There is also a particularly puzzling passage in *De Anima* II, 1, section 412a, which runs:

> It is also uncertain whether the psyche as an actuality bears the same relation to the body as the sailor to a ship.

The idea of the psyche as an *inhabitant* of the body does not, as far as I know, appear elsewhere in Aristotle.

Note 2.11. *De Rerum Natura*, Book V, lines 148 and 150 (R.E. Latham's translation, Penguin 1951).

Note 2.12. *De Rerum Natura*, Book III, lines 94 seq.

Note 2.13. *De Rerum Natura*, Book I, lines 265 seq.

Note 2.14. *De Rerum Natura*, Book I, lines 62-79. The Latin word which Latham translates as 'superstition' is in fact 'religio'.

Note 2.15. *Genesis* **ii**, 7. The Hebrew word translated here as 'soul' means literally 'breath'. The translators into Greek used 'psyche'.

Note 2.16. *Ezekiel* **xxxvii**, 8 and 9

Note 2,17. *Exodus* **xx**, 5.

Note 2.18. *Psalm* **xcix**, 1.

Note 2.19. *Isaiah* **xl**, 15.

Note 2.20. *Isaiah* **vi**, 5.

Note 2.21. *Psalm* **xiv**, 1 (compare Psalm liii, 1).

Note 2.22. *John* **i**, 1-14.

Note 2.23. *Mark* **xii**, 30 (compare Luke x, 27).

Note 2.24 *Matthew* **x**, 28.

Note 2.25. *1 Corinthians* **xv**, 37 seq.

Note 2.26. *Hebrews* **xi**, 1

Note 2.27. *2 Corinthians* **iv**, 18

Note 2.28. *Romans* **viii**, 5.

NOTES TO CHAPTER 3

Note 3.1. *Cruden's Complete Concordance to the Old and New Testaments*, by Alexander Cruden. Guildford: Lutterworth Press, 1974.

Note 3.2. *A Complete Concordance of the Dramatic Works and Poems of Shakespeare*, by John Bartlett. London: Macmillan, 1894.

Note 3.3. R. Descartes, *Tract on Man*.

Note 3.4. R. Descartes, *Discourse on Method*, Part IV.

Note 3.5. I. Kant, *Critique of Pure Reason*, Preface to the second edition.

Note 3.6. See especially Kant's *Critique of Pure Reason*, Transcendental Dialectic. Among 18th-century philosophers it seems to me that Berkeley and Kant were among the foremost in demonstrating that the closed system implicit in the world picture of Newtonian physics did not have unwelcome implications for religion and morality.

Note 3.7. G. Ryle, *The Concept of Mind*. London: Hutchinson, 1949, p.20.

Note 3.8. Even so eminent a scientist as Sir John Eccles in his discussions of behaviourism seems to me to have resorted to attacking a man of straw, as the following passage shows:

> At the zenith (or nadir!) of the influence of Ryle's challenging book, *The Concept of Mind* (1949), such words as mind, consciousness, thoughts, purposes, beliefs were not allowable... All words savouring of Cartesian

dualism became 'dirty' words, unallowable in 'polite' philosophical discourse. Ironically the most prominent philosophical obscenities were a new class of four-letter words – mind, self, soul, will'. (See J.C. Eccles, *Evolution of the Brain: Creation of the Self*, London: Routledge 1989, p.225).

I know of no philosopher who has proposed that the 'mentalistic' words mentioned by Eccles should never be used. Ryle was concerned with what he interestingly called their 'logical geography' (see G. Ryle, *The Concept of Mind*, London: Hutchinson, 1949, p.7). There are, I suspect, others who profess to disagree with Ryle; given his methods of philosophising, however, which can appropriately be characterised as 'conceptual analysis', it is hard to see what these apparent philosophical opponents think they are disagreeing with him about!

Note 3.9. G. Ryle, *The Concept of Mind*. London: Hutchinson, 1949, p.11.

Note 3.10. Various versions of this limerick seem to be in circulation. The version quoted here will be found in *The Faber Book of Comic Verse* (ed. Michael Roberts), London: Faber & Faber, 1990, p.327.

NOTES TO CHAPTER 4

Note 4.1. George Berkeley, *Second Dialogue between Hylas and Philonous.*

Note 4.2. J.L. Austin, *Sense and Sensibilia*. Oxford: Oxford University Press, 1962. Even in as scholarly a work as *Is God Real?*, ed. Joseph Runzo (London: Macmillan, 1993) some of the participants seem to assume that the word 'real' raises no problems.

Note 4.3. For a very readable account of what has been called the 'verification principle' see A.J. Ayer, *Language, Truth, and Logic* (London: Gollancz, 1949). It is agreed that there are many difficulties in Ayer's original formulation, but the central idea – viz. that if one is making a claim on a matter of fact one needs to specify what is the 'pay off' observation – seems to me to be valid. It is a logical point which follows from the commonly understood meaning of the word 'fact'; and while it is not in dispute that changing the meaning of words so that they have a different logic is a legitimate activity, there is the risk that one may mislead oneself or use words in a self-defeating way. Other ways of making the same point are to say that one must always be willing to give one's words 'cash value' (compare William James, *Varieties of Religious Experience*. London: Longmans Green & Co., 1941, p.443) or to indicate how the words in question are to be 'operationally defined' (see P.W. Bridgman, *The Logic of Modern Physics*. London: Macmillan, 1927. A further interesting discussion of these issues will be found in F. Waismann, 'Verifiability'. *Aristotelian Society*, Supplementary Volume xix, 1945, reprinted in A.G.N. Flew (ed.) *Logic and Language* (first series). Blackwell, Oxford, 1950. Waismann raises in particular the issue of what counts as conclusive verification. To make a claim that there is a cat in the room, for instance, is it enough to see the cat or does one have to induce it to purr? He refers in this connection to the 'open texture' of language; this means in effect that the question of what is the decisive specification is left somewhat open.

Although the verification principle has tended to be ignored in recent years I know of no valid grounds for challenging its basic insight. To place restrictions on what can and cannot be said – when there may be all kinds of different reasons for saying it – would indeed be foolhardy and doctrinaire; but as a matter of logic those who claim to be making factual statements are thereby committed to making specifications of *some* kind.

In this connection it seems to me possible that when Laplace (in answer to a questioner who asked if he had discovered God in the skies) produced his famous remark, 'Je n'ai besoin de cet hypothèse' he was intentionally been ironic. He was not saying, 'The God-hypothesis is *false*' but indicating by innuendo that the existence of God was not a hypothesis at all.

Note 4.4. G. Ryle, *The Concept of Mind*. London: Hutchinson, 1949, Chapter 5.

NOTES TO CHAPTER 5

Note 5.1. Anselm, *Proslogion*, II (see pp. 116-7 of M.J. Charlesworth's translation and commentary. Clarendon Press, 1965).

Note 5.2. St. Thomas Aquinas, *Summa Theologiae*, vol.2, 1a, 3.

Note 5.3. W.I. Matson, *The Existence of God*. Cornell: Cornell University Press, 1965, p.xi. I am grateful to Martin Warner for calling my attention to this passage.

Note 5.4. ibid. p.xi.

Note 5.5. ibid. p.xiii. Matson goes on to say that

> the difficult questions are those concerned with what would *count* as evidence for the conclusion... Roughly speaking, the difficulties in our enquiry will be with points of logic, not of fact' (ibid. p.13).

This is unexceptionable. The problem, however, is

that it is not clear how *any* evidence could establish, or even

make probable, the 'existence of God' in the sense which Matson

has in mind.

Note 5.6. Richard Swinburne, *The Existence of God* (Revised Edition) Oxford: Clarendon Press, 1991, p.8

Note 5.7. H.W. Montefiore, *The Probability of God*. London: SCM Press, 1985.

Note 5.8. J.J.C. Smart and J.J. Haldane, *Atheism and Theism*. Oxford: Blackwell, 1996.

Note 5.9. Compare J. McQuarrie, *In Search of Deity*. London: SCM Press, 1984, p.23:

> Who ever addressed a prayer to a necessary being?

Note 5.10. Keith Ward, *God, Chance and Necessity*. Oxford: Oneworld Publications, 1996.

Note 5.11. Some religious believers may be tempted to echo the words which come in Virgil's *Aeneid* (Book 2, line 521):

> Non tali auxilio nec defensoribus istis ('not such succour nor such defenders').

Note 5.12. In this connection I cannot resist quoting a comment made by Kant (*Critique of Pure Reason*, Transcendental Logic) on what happens when questions are asked which are logically inappropriate:

To know what questions we may reasonably propose is in itself a strong evidence of sagacity and intelligence. For if a question be in itself absurd and unsusceptible of a rational answer, it is attended with the danger – not to mention the shame that falls upon the person who proposes it – of seducing the unguarded listener into making absurd answers, and we are presented with the ridiculous spectacle of one (as the ancients said) 'milking a he-goat, and the other holding a sieve'.

Note 5.13 For a discussion of the distinction between 'lexical' and 'stipulative' definitions see Richard Robinson, *Definition* (Oxford: Oxford University Press, 1950). Mention should also be made of the expression 'persuasive definition' which was used in particular by C.L. Stevenson (see his *Ethics and Language*, Yale: Yale University Press, 1944). The present book is offering what in Stevenson's terminology would be called a 'persuasive' definition – in this case of the word 'religion'. That is to say, I am urging (or trying to 'persuade') the reader to view religious language in a particular way.

Note 5.14. *Job* **xiii**, 15.

Note 5.15. *Job* **ii**, 9.

Note 5.16. A very interesting discussion of the way in which religious commitment needs to be unconditional will be found in R.M. Hare, Theology and falsification, B. (see Antony Flew and Alasdair Macintyre (eds.), *New Essays in Philosophical Theology*. London: SCM Press, 1955). Hare's paper provides a striking demonstration of how (in my terminology) it is possible to be a committed Christian without subscribing to the 'Magnus' image.

Note 5.17. *The Book of Common Prayer*, Solemnization of Matrimony.

Note 5.18. D. Cupitt, *Taking Leave of God*. London: SCM Press, 1980, pp. 136-137.

Note 5.19. The technical word for this kind of enquiry is 'negative' (or 'apophatic') theology. See also note 7.12.

Note 5.20 For particularly interesting uses of this technique see George Berkeley, *Three Dialogues between Hylas and Philonous*. There is also a reference to it in Berkeley's *Alciphron*, where Alciphron, who is described as a 'free thinker', says to his audience:

> I am very sensible that eyes long kept in the dark cannot bear a sudden view of noonday light, but must be brought to it by degrees. It is for this reason the ingenious gentlemen of our profession are accustomed to proceed gradually, beginning with those prejudices to which men have the least attachment, and thence proceeding to undermine the rest by slow and insensible degrees, till they have demolished the whole fabric of human folly and superstition (see George Berkeley, *Alciphron*, ed. David Berman. London: Routledge, 1993, p.31).

It is also interesting to note that when St. Paul visited Athens he did not rush in with the message that Jesus, the Messiah, had been crucified – presumably because this would have totally bewildered his audience since they were not expecting a messiah! Instead he began by commending their religious scrupulousness and attempted to build on what was already meaningful for them.

Note 5.21. *Genesis* **vi**, 6.

Note 5.22. Christopher Marlowe, *The Tragical History of Doctor Faustus*.

Note 5.23. See in particular *John* **iii**, 16.

Note 5.24. *Hymns Ancient and Modern* no. 578. The author is Mrs Dorothy Gurney.

Note 5.25 Keith Ward, Is God a person? In: *Christian Faith and Philosophical Theology* (pp. 259-260), ed. Gijsbert van den Brink, Luco J. van den Brom, and Marcel Sarot (Essays in Honour of Vincent Brummer). The Netherlands: Pharos Publishing House, 1992.

Note 5.26. For an account of language acquisition along these lines see B.F. Skinner, *Verbal Behaviour*. New York: Appleton Century Crofts, 1957.

Note 5.27. Ward, op.cit. pp.259-260. See also the start of chapter 4 and note 4.1.

NOTES TO CHAPTER 6

Note 6.1 L. Wittgenstein, *Philosophical Investigations* (tr. G.E.M. Anscombe), Blackwell, Oxford, *passim*.

Note 6.2. Don Cupitt, *Taking Leave of God*. London: SCM Press, 1980, p.122.

Note 6.3. In lighter vein I cannot forbear quoting a story told me by the late Canon L.W. Grensted. When archbishop William Temple had written on the theme of *'mens creatrix'* ('creative mind') a proof reader – presumably not well versed in the latin language – inserted an apostrophe between the 'n' and the 's' of *mens*. As a result the text read 'men's creatrix' – as it might be, men's female creator!

Note 6.4. A very interesting exploitation of this analogy will be found in John Wisdom's paper, Gods. See his *Philosophy and Psychoanalysis*, Blackwell: Oxford, 1953, pp.149-168.

NOTES TO CHAPTER 7

Note 7.1. The notion of 'really believing' is problematic. People may *say* they believe things as a result of self-deception or sometimes with deliberate intent to mislead; and, in standard cases, what entitles us to say that they do not 'really' believe it is that they act in ways that are totally inconsistent with these professed beliefs. A brilliantly mischievous paper has been written by D.Z. Phillips entitled 'On really believing', in which he pokes fun at so-called 'philosophical realists' for indulging in 'philosophy by italics'.

> We are told that we would not worship unless we believed that God *exists*. We are told that we cannot talk to God unless he is *there* to talk to. We are told that, for the believer, God's existence is a *fact*. And so on. But nothing is achieved by italicising these words. The task of clarifying their grammar when they are used remains' (see *Is God Real?*, ed. Joseph Runzo, London, Macmillan, 1993, p.87).

It is hard to see what sense can be attached to the expression 'really believing in God' unless 'Magnus' ways of thinking are assumed.

Note 7.2. *Yes, Prime Minister: The Diaries of the Right Hon. James Hacker,* ed. Jonathan Lynn and Antony Jay, BBC Publications, 1986.

Note 7.3. *The Myth of God Incarnate* (ed. John Hick). London: SCM Press, 1977.

Note 7.4. *The Truth of God Incarnate* (ed. Michael Green). London: Hodder & Stoughton, 1977.

Note 7.5. See, for instance, John Hick, *The Metaphor of God Incarnate.* London: SCM Press, 1993.

Note 7.6. Richard Braithwaite, *An Empiricist's View of the Nature of Religious Belief.* Cambridge: Cambridge University Press, 1955.

Note 7.7. ibid. p.27.

Note 7.8. It is reported that on one occasion Professor Braithwaite put forward the views expressed in *An Empiricist's View of the Nature of Religious Belief* to members of a philosophical group in Oxford and at the end of his talk asked his audience to vote on whether or not he should be counted as a Christian. The outcome, so I am told, was that most of the Christians in the audience said that he was a Christian and most of the non-Christians that he was not. On this occasion it seems to me that the Christians were being more perceptive, since, unlike the non-Christians, they were in effect recognising that Christianity need not be tied to the Magnus image!

Note 7.9. T.R. Miles, *Religion and the Scientific Outlook.* London: Allen & Unwin, 1959.

Note 7.10. T. Hobbes, *Leviathan,* Part 1, chapter 13.

Note 7.11. J.J. Rousseau, *The Social Contract,* Book 1, chapter 1.

Note 7.12. *Genesis* chapters 1 and 2. When I discussed these issues with a clergyman friend recently he said, 'Of course I believe that the story of Adam and Eve is a myth. But I would think it most unwise to say so in the pulpit for fear of its being misunderstood.' I know of another clergyman who told me that he used the technique of what he called 'outrageous literalism': he spoke of God, Adam, Eve, the serpent, etc. all in human terms, implicitly, though not explicitly, making clear that it was the religious message, not the literal truth, which he regarded as important.

Note 7.13. For further information on apophatic theology see in particular B. McGinn, *The Foundations of Mysticism*, London: SCM Press, 1991. I am grateful to Dr Oliver Davies for calling my attention to this work.

Note 7.14. H.D. Lewis, The cognitive factor in religious experience. *Aristotelian Society*, Supplementary Volume XXIX, 1955.

Note 7.15. Scotus Erigena, *De Divisione Naturae*, Book I, chapter 73.

Note 7.16. *Acts* **xvii**, 34.

Note 7.17. For sources for the next three quotations see Pseudo-Dionysius, *The Complete Works*. London: SPCK, 1987. The first quotation is from *The Mystical Theology*, 3, 1033C, p.139.

Note 7.18. *The Mystical Theology*, 5, 1048B, p.141.

Note 7.19 *The Celestial Hierarchy*, 2, 141A, pp.149-150..

Note 7.20 *Meister Eckhart* by Franz Pfeiffer, trans. C de B. Evans. London: John M. Watkins 1920, p.148. I am grateful to Lorna Marsden for having called my attention to this passage and the two which follow.

Note 7.21. Nicholas of Cusa, *Letter to Albergati*, 1463.

Note 7.22. F. Hartmann, *Jacob Boehme*. London: Kegan Paul, Trench & Trubner, 1891.

Note 7.23. I have been unable to trace this quotation which I believe owes its origin to Kirkegaard.

NOTES TO CHAPTER 8

Note 8.1. I cannot resist at this point telling two light-hearted stories. I hope they will not offend. The first is of a pastor who was ministering to a tribe in the desert. As there had been a severe drought he was asked to pray for rain, which he duly did. Next day it rained – and then the next day after that, and the next... and the next! The rain started to flood them out, and finally, therefore, the pastor was asked to pray that the rain would stop. He did so, using the following words: 'O Lord, we prayed for rain and you have given us rain – but *do* be reasonable!'

The second story tells of a clergyman who was walking in a town and who heard a succession of profanities emanating from the next street. When he walked there he discovered a lorry driver trying desperately – but unsuccessfully – to start his lorry with the cranking handle. He therefore went up to him and said, 'My friend, what is the trouble?' In reply the driver gave vent to some further profanities, saying, 'I have been here twenty ----- minutes and I can't get my ---------- ----- lorry to start!' The clergyman then said: 'Shall we try a little prayer?' Said the lorry driver, 'I have been here twenty ---- minutes and I'll try any ---- ----- thing'. So the clergyman said a prayer, and, when he had finished, the driver once more turned the cranking handle. This time the lorry started instantly. He therefore jumped into the cab, waved a cheerful 'good-bye' to the clergyman and drove off. The clergyman stared after him in amazement, muttering to himself, 'Well, I'll be damned'!

Note 8.2. For further discussion of this and related issues about the efficacy of prayer see Vincent Brummer, *What Are We Doing When We Pray?* London: SCM Press, 1984.

Note 8.3. See Francis Galton, 'Objective efficiency of prayer', in *Inquiries into Human Faculty and Its Development*, London: Macmillan, 1883, pp.277 seq.)

Note 8.4. See T.R. Miles, *Religion and the Scientific Outlook*. London: Allen·& Unwin, 1959), chapter 11.

Note 8.5. Helen Oppenheimer, cited in Brummer (op.cit. note 8.2, p.55).

Note 8.6. See J.L. Austin, Other Minds, in *Aristotelian Society*, Supplementary Volume XX for 1946, p.173.

Note 8.7. Te deum laudamus. *The Book of Common Prayer*, Morning Prayer.

Note 8.8. *Luke* **viii**, 13.

Note 8.9. I am grateful to Vincent Brummer (op. cit., note 8.2) for his thoughtful discussion of what I said about prayer in my *Religion and the Scientific Outlook* (London: Allen & Unwin, 1959). However it was not my intention in that book to justify the practice of prayer on the grounds of the benefits which may sometimes accrue to the person praying. In the language of the present book such prayers would not involve unconditional commitment and would not therefore count as 'religious'. What I would wish to say is that there can be value in the performance of a ritual regardless of any benefits either to the person carrying out the ritual or the person being prayed for.

Note 8.10. That one should always be prepared to specify what would count *against* a particular hypothesis is widely agreed to be a basic requirement of scientific method (see in particular K. Popper, *Conjectures and Refutations*, London: Routledge & Kegan Paul, 1963, especially p.36).

NOTES TO CHAPTER 9

Note 9.1. These actual words will be found in C.S. Lewis' book, *Miracles: A Preliminary Study*, (London: Geoffrey Bles, 1947, p.15). In C.S. Lewis's writings on religion it seems to me in general that 'Magnus' ways of thinking loom uncomfortably large.

Note 9.2. I have chosen this example because I actually heard it used by an army chaplain in the early part of the second world war. My recollection is that I felt at the time there was 'something wrong' with what was being claimed and that somehow God was 'not like that'. My exposure of Magnus in this book can perhaps be seen as an attempt, over fifty years on, to make explicit what it was about the claim that caused my unease.

Note 9.3 Kant in his *Critique of Pure Reason* argued that humans are so made that they necessarily organise their perception of the world in certain ways – there cannot be 'gaps' in the chain of causation (see in particular the section entitled 'Refutation of idealism': *in mundo non datur hiatus, non datur saltus*). Compare also the following interesting passage from Wittgenstein's *Philosophical Investigations*, Oxford: Blackwell, 1953, section 52.

> If I am inclined to suppose that a mouse has come into being by spontaneous generation out of grey rags and dust, I shall do well to examine those rags very closely to see how a mouse may have hidden in them, how it may have got there and so on. But if I am convinced

that a mouse cannot come into being from these things, then this investigation will perhaps be superfluous.

In lighter vein I should like also to mention a radio broadcast which I heard recently. I did not note the exact words, but it seems that an actress was scheduled to perform the part of Leda when she was visited by Zeus in the form of a swan. 'He flapped his wings round me, and *I do not remember what happened next*' (my italics). I am mischievously tempted to pose the question, Just what *could* have happened next?

Note 9.4. For a critique of the mind-matter dichotomy see in particular G. Ryle, *The Concept of Mind*. London: Hutchinson, 1949. Compare the discussion in chapter 3 of this book.

Note 9.5. See, for instance, *Matthew* **vii**, 22; *Mark* **vi**, 5, and *John* **iii**, 2. An interesting view which argues both for the historicity and the symbolic significance of the gospel miracle stories was put forward by Drusilla Scott (*The Times*, Jan. 5th 1985):

> 14 scientists... wrote that they all gladly accepted the gospel miracles, for 'miracles are unprecedented events... science, based as it is on observation and precedents, can have nothing to say on the subject. Its laws are only generalizations of our experience'. ... I can imagine these 14 scientists watching a pig with wings flying round the garden, saying to each other (quite calm and unastonished), 'That's interesting, we have not observed that before'. Of course that is not what they would say; they would either think that a clever trick was being played or that they were hallucinating. For the pig would not simply be unprecedented but incredible.

Scott goes on to say,

> A miracle points to a hidden meaning, and the profundity of the meaning can make the miracle believable.

Note 9.6. This is an argument of the type which logicians call 'reductio ad absurdum' (if p then q; not q, therefore not p). Such arguments are regularly misunderstood – a point which I should like to illustrate by means of a cautionary tale. Some years ago an eminent Oxford don had occasion to discuss certain philosophical views about the purpose of punishment, in particular the thesis that its principle aim ought to be that of deterring others from committing similar offences. He pointed out that if this account of the aims of punishment were correct one would be committed to advocating the execution of those convicted of dangerous driving. – since this would certainly act as a deterrent! His intention, of course, was to show that a 'deterrence' theory of the purpose of punishment was inadequate since it ignored the question of whether such a punishment was 'fair' or 'deserved'. However he was execrated in some quarters on the grounds that he had advocated the execution of dangerous drivers! The mistake is precisely similar to that made by people who attribute to David Jenkins the view that the resurrection was 'nothing more than a conjuring trick with bones'. Such are the pitfalls of the *reductio ad absurdum* argument.

Note 9.7. *John* **iii**, 30

Note 9.8. *John* **ix**, 25

Note 9.9. *John* **xviii**, 34.

Note 9.10. The following passage written by Derek Stanesby (*The Times*, Dec. 12th 1987) seems worth quoting in this connection:

> The theological point is that the birth of Jesus marked a new beginning in the story of creation...These ideas were naturally developed in the light of the ancient understanding of human reproduction. What do we make of them in the light of a more informed contemporary account of biological evolution and of reproductive processes? Presumably the virginal conception involved one of two possibilities. Either Mary was simply a vessel containing and nourishing the divinely implanted seed, that is, a surrogate mother, or she provided the ovum for impregnation by the Holy Ghost and so contributed to her son's genetic inheritance'.

This seems to me an ingenious attempt to answer the question, What actually happened? However it is arguable that there is something absurd about such speculations and that what is important is not the biological facts but the mythos which the story of the virgin birth embodies.

Note 9.11. William Munro, writing in *The Times*, February 16th, 1985.

NOTES TO CHAPTER 10

Note 10.1. *Genesis* **i**, 1-3.

Note 10.2. According to Kant there are valid arguments to show both that the world had a beginning in time and that it did not (see *The Critique of Pure Reason*, Antinomies of Pure Reason). We are so made that we experience events as laid out in space and as successive in time; as a result we cannot conceive of *limits* to space or time or of a 'first cause' at the start of the temporal series. Compare also a fascinating passage in Lucretius (*De Rerum Natura*, Book 1, lines 958 seq.) which contains the following:

> Whatever spot anyone may occupy, the universe stretches away from him in all directions without limit. Suppose for a moment that the whole of space were bounded and that someone made his way to the uttermost boundary and threw a flying dart. Do you choose to suppose that the missile, hurled with might and main, would speed along the course on which it was aimed? Or do you think something would block the way and stop it? You must assume one alternative or the other. But neither of them leaves you a loophole. Both force you to admit that the universe continues without end (R.E. Latham's translation).

Note 10.3 *Church Quarterly Review*, January-March, 1955.

Note 10.4 George Berkeley, *Third Dialogue Between Hylas and Philonous*. The passage continues as follows:

> I say moreover, that in this naked conception of things, divested of words, there will not be found any notion of what you call the *actuality of absolute existence*. You may indeed raise a dust with these terms, and so lengthen our dispute to no purpose. But I entreat you calmly to look into your own thoughts, and then tell me if they are not an useless and unintelligible jargon.

Despite what some critics have supposed, it seems to me clear that Berkeley thought of himself not as the proponent of a highly speculative theory but as a defender of common sense, his aim being in effect to rid people of the high-faluting jargon which had been imposed on both philosophy and religion by some of the learned thinkers of his time. I sometimes feel that present-day philosophy of religion is in danger of suffering from the same malady.

Note 10.5. *Oxford Dictionary of the Christian Church*. Oxford: Oxford University Press, p.1182.

Note 10.6. From *Aristotle*, by A.E. Taylor. London: Dodge Publishing Co., 1912, p.48.

Note 10.7. *Oxford Dictionary of the Christian Church*. Oxford: Oxford University Press, p.684.

Note 10.8. J.A.T. Robinson, *Honest to God*. London: SCM Press, 1963, p.66.

Note 10.9. *Acts* **xiv**, 11-12.

Note 10.10. See the hymn, 'Earth has many a noble city', *Hymns Ancient and Modern*, no.76. The English version is by E. Caswall and others; the original latin version was by Prudentius (348-c.413).

Note 10.11. *John* **i**, 14.

Note 10.12. *Oxford Dictionary of the Christian Church*. Oxford: Oxford University Press, p.465.

Note 10.13. Christopher Marlowe, *The Tragical History of Doctor Faustus*.

Note 10.14. From 'On the resurrection morning' by S. Baring-Gould. *Hymns Ancient and Modern*, no.499.

Note 10.15. As was noted in chapter 2, when a warrior died in the Trojan war his psyche 'took wing for Hades'. This was clearly not thought of as the departure of something 'immaterial' in the post-16th century sense.

Note 10.16. J.V. Langmead Casserley, *The Retreat from Christianity in the Modern World*, London: Longmans, 1952, p.24.

Note 10.17. *John* **x**, 28.

Note 10.18. *John* **xi**, 25-26.

Note 10.19. 'Hell', by Ian Ramsey. In *Talk of God*. Royal Institute of Philosophy Lectures, volume 2, 1967-8.

Note 10.20. *Talk of God*, op. cit. pp.222-225.

Note 10.21. I cannot resist ending this discussion of hell in a more lighthearted vein. The following gem was supplied to me by my friend, Evelyn Evans, though she does not vouch for its authenticity:

> At the evening service tonight the sermon will be 'What is hell?' Come early and listen to our choir.

Note 10.22. *Oxford Dictionary of the Christian Church*. Oxford: Oxford University Press, p.101.

Note 10.23. I owe this analogy to Professor Donald Mackinnon.

Note 10.24. *Romans* **iii**, 23.

Note 10.25. *Romans* **vi**, 23.

Note 10.26. 'Guidance by the holy spirit' and 'following the leadings of the holy spirit' are also expressions which occur in a number of religious contexts. Interpreted in 'Magnus' terms they seemingly imply that some non-physical agency is at work which steers people's decisions in a particular direction; interpreted (as they should be) as profound truth their function is to emphasise the need for the total abandonment of 'self' in any process of decision making.

Note 10.27. *Ephesians* **ii**, 8.

Note 10.28. 'Sweet saviour, bless us ere we go', by F.W. Faber. *Hymns Ancient and Modern*, no. 28.

Note 10.29. 'Rock of ages, cleft for me', by A.M. Toplady. *Hymns Ancient and Modern*, no. 184.

Note 10.30. *Hamlet*, Act II, scene 1.

NOTES TO CHAPTER 11

Note 11.1. For a telling discussion of this point see C.S. Lewis, *The Problem of Pain*, London: Geoffrey Bles, 1956, Chapter 1.

Note 11.2. George Berkeley, *Third Dialogue between Hylas and Philonous*.

Note 11.3. *Romans* **vi**, 9.

Note 11.4. *Habakkuk* **i**, 13.

Note 11.5. *Psalm* **xxxvii**, 36.

Note 11.6. *Psalm* **xxxvii**, 25.

Note 11.7. Many years ago, as part of my training as a psychologist, I had the opportunity to visit a hospital for the very severely mentally handicapped. These were fellow human beings, yet they seemed like *wrecks* of humanity – many of them severely brain damaged and few of them, despite the dedicated attentions of their carers, in a position to derive any enjoyment from life. My reaction afterwards was in part one of indignation – 'Why has God done this?' I mention this experience not for the sake of being autobiographical but as an illustration of a religious response – a response in profound language – to the existence of what seemed like wholly undeserved suffering.

NOTES TO CHAPTER 12

Note 12.1. *The Book of Common Prayer*, A General Thanksgiving.

Note 12.2. *Psalm* **xix**, 1

Note 12.3. *Macbeth*, Act 5, scene 5.

Note 12.4. Lewis Carroll, *Through the Looking Glass*, chapter 5.

Note 12.5. It has been pointed out to me by Don Cupitt that there are relatively few occasions in the new testament when '*pisteuein hoti*' ('believe that') is used, but many more when the words are '*pisteuein en*' ('believe in'). The essential feature of 'pistis' (from which 'pisteuein' is derived) is that of 'trust' or 'faith', and this is also true of the latin word 'credo' from which 'creed' is derived. The translation of 'pistis' and 'credo' as 'belief', with the implication of 'believing *that*' rather than 'trusting *in*' has, I am sure, played its part in promoting 'Magnus' ways of thinking. 'I believe in God', as it occurs at the start of the apostles' creed, is a declaration of trust, not a declaration that one believes that certain facts are the case.

Note 12.6. Stephen Mitchell, *Sea of Faith Magazine*, no.18, July 1994, p.3.

Note 12.7. A striking exception is a paper written by J.N. Findlay (see *Mind*, LVII, 226, 1948, 176-183). Findlay's argument is complex, but the following passages convey something of its flavour:

Having described a worshipful attitude as one in which we feel disposed to bend the knee before some object, to defer to it wholly, and the like, we find it natural to say that such an attitude can only be fitting where the object reverenced *exceeds* us very vastly... Hence we are led on irresistably to demand that our religious object should have an *unsurpassable* supremacy along all avenues, that it should tower *infinitely* above all other objects... We can't help feeling that the worthy object of our worship can never be a thing which merely *happens* to exist, nor one on which all other objects merely *happen* to depend.

Professor Findlay then goes on to argue that if such a being is to be an object of worship he must by definition be thought of asd a *necessary* being; however, as a matter of logic, it is not possible for any statement of the form 'X exists' to be necessary. He therefore concludes that the idea of a necessary being existing is incoherent. In commenting on Findlay's paper George Hughes questions the validity of his argument and mischievously refers to it as an 'ontological disproof' of God's existence (see *Mind*, LVIII, 229, 1949, 67-74).

Note 12.8. As a very interesting book on atheism I particularly recommend Richard Robinson's *An Atheist's Values*. Oxford: Blackwell, 1964.

Note 12.9. *The Independent*, 3rd September 1996.

Note 12.10. I owe this phrase to Bruce Findlow who used it in a letter to *The Times* (7th January 1984).

Index

110

ORIGEN, 61

Paranormal phenomena, 52
PAUL (St.), 68, 96
Petitionary prayer, 47-54
Performatory language, 55, 100
Persuasive definition, 95
PFEIFFER, F., 99
PHILLIPS, D.Z., viii, 97
PLATO, 10, 90
POPPER, K., 101
PRUDENTIUS, 105
PSEUDO-DIONYSIUS, ii, 44, 99
Psychokinesis, 10, 52

Quakers (Society of Friends), vii, 50
Questionnaires, use of, 83

RAMSAY, I.T., viii, 71, 72, 88, 106
Real, reality, 20, 21
Realism, 88, 89, 97
Relativism, 84, 85
Resurrection, 59 (*see also* Eternal life)
Revelåtion, 66, 67
RICHARDS, G., viii
ROBERTS, M., 92
ROBINSON, J.A.T., vi, vii, viii, 67, 68, 87, 105
ROUSSEAU, J.J., 43, 98
RUNZO, R., 92, 97.
RUSSELL, B., 28, 29
RYLE, G., viii, 1, 17, 18, 87, 89, 92, 93, 102

SAROT, M., 96
SAMKARA, 44
SCOTT, D., 102
SCOTUS ERIGENA, 44, 99

SHAKESPEARE, W., 15
SKINNER, B.F., 96
SMART, J.J.C., 29, 94
Social contract, 93
STANESBURY, D., 103
STEVENSON, C.L., 95
Stipulative definition, 95
STOPES-ROE, H., 84
SWINBURNE, R., 28, 94

TAYLOR, A.E., 66, 67, 105
TEMPLE, W., 97
TOPLADY, A.M., 106
Transference situation, 51
TLC (tender loving care), 51

VAN DEN BRINK, G., 96
VAN DEN BROM, L., 96
Verification principle, 25, 42, 53, 54, 92, 93
VIRGIL, 94
Virgin birth, 59, 60, 68, 103

WAISMANN, F., 93
WARNER, M., viii, 94
WELDON, T.D., 8, 89
Whipping boy (theories of atonement), 73
WILLIAMS, J.M.G., viii
WISDOM, J., 97
WITTGENSTEIN, L., 35, 38, 97, 101, 102
WODEHOUSE, P.G., 4, 88
WYNN PARRY, D., viii

York, R., viii

111